GRANDMA'S MURDER CLUB

TM

A Stage Play In Two Acts

by
Kathy McSteen

Adapted from the Film "Bad Grandmas"
written by
Srikant Chellappa and Jack Snyder

Published by Florida Comedy Network LLC

"Grandmas" graphic by Leslie Weed
Designedby-Leslie.com

GRANDMA'S MURDER CLUB

Mimi and Coralee's plans to save their friend, Bobbi, from more tragedy after her daughter's untimely death go "caddy-wonked." They kill a bad guy to save themselves--then his partners show up. Older and wiser wins the day as they fill a freezer, dodge a detective, find romance, and rescue Bobbi. Mimi's grandson shares their secrets and leaves you laughing as the love and support of good friends shines strong in Kathy McSteen's comic adaptation of Florence Henderson's last film which also featured Pamela Grier, Judge Reinhold and Randall Batinkoff.

Florida Comedy Network LLC

ISBN: 978-0-578-30205-8

A traditionally formatted play script is available separately. You may request a complimentary copy for production consideration by email to:

FloridaComedyNetwork@gmail.com

Include your your full name, theatre association, title, and phone number.

As part of a production contract, you will receive a digital file of authorized music and "stingers" from the movie "Bad Grandmas," as well as sound effects and sign graphics.

We hope you and your audience enjoy the play's quirky Witchee Twitchee FL characters, including the resourceful friends "of a certain age." The playwright supports flexibility in the actors' ages, ethnicity, and gender.

6 Actors

COLBY POWELL..............20s-30s, Mimi's affable son, Colby becomes JIM's RECEPTIONIST, the GROCERY STORE MANAGER, NEIGHBOR BOY, and his grandmother's nemesis, HARRY BLEVINS, transitioning on stage with minimal costume elements.

MIMI DOOLEY...................50s to 80s. Colby's down-to-earth, practical grandmother.

CORALEE CAMPBELL...... 50s to 80s. Mimi's physically large, force-of-nature friend.

BOBBI ROSE................... 50s to 80s. Mimi's snobbish, acerbic friend.

JIM MCCAUSEY/STAN.......30s to 40s, Bobbi's callous white collar son-in-law. After his last appearance, the actor becomes Harry's second banana employee Stan—a comically sweet dim bulb who turns sour in this dual role. Role can be split.

RANDALL MCCLEMORE... 50s to 80s. A small-town detective formerly from Texas.

PLACE: Whitchee Twitchee Florida, a small central Florida town

TIME: Early in the 2000s and back when Colby was younger.

Set Notes: The set as originally conceived includes Jim's Office and Mimi's Kitchen on opposite sides from each other with an upstage center door between them. There are also stage right and left exits at the upstage and downstage corners. The downstage area is available for use as other "places."

Mimi's Kitchen includes a window, a table and three chairs, a chest style freezer, vacuum cleaner, frying pan hanging by the door, and a counter or small table or shelf for props.

Jim's Office includes a narrow table or desk, a rolling and a stationary chair, and an "Orange Blossom Insurance Agency" sign.

There is a hat rack or shelf for Colby's (the narrator) props and costume elements in a downstage corner.

After Jim "dies," his office can become the Auto Shop by pushing the desk against the side wall, moving the chairs in front of the desk, adding a few garage worthy pin-ups to the upstage area, and flipping over the insurance agency sign (or replacing it) to read "Bump and Grind Auto Shop."

Using this format, no furniture is moved off and on stage, speeding up scene transitions. Action takes place at times on both sides of the stage during a scene.

GRANDMA'S MURDER CLUB's staged reading took place at The Lemon Bay Playhouse in Englewood, FL, on June 19, 2021. Jeff Dillon-- Director, Set, and Lighting Design; Pauleen Logsdon, Stage Manager; Robert LaSalle, Technical Director; Lori Sigrist, Production and Artistic Director. The cast in order of appearance was as follows:

COLBY...Tyler Joseph Colfer
MIMI...Judy Tilley
BOBBI..Judy Glynn
CORALEE..Trish Campbell
JIM/STAN...Logan Light
RANDY...Gene Callan

GRANDMA'S MURDER CLUB was first produced at the Cultural Park Theatre, Cape Coral, FL on January 24, 2025. Robin Murray, Director, Costume, and Sound Design; Chris Murray, Set Design; Austin Murray, Technical Director; Nicole Krokosz, Stage Manager. The cast in order of appearance was as follows.

COLBY...Max Rousseau
MIMI...Whitney Taylor
BOBBI..Donna Richman
CORALEE..Eileen Haas-Linde
JIM/STAN...John Strealy
RANDY...Will House

ACT I

Scene 1

At Rise: We see Jim's Office and Mimi's Kitchen. Cheerful music plays as COLBY enters and greets the audience.

COLBY. Evening! Hi, y'all. How you doin' tonight? Feeling good, I hope! You're looking great. Glad to see you! I'm Colby, Colby Powell. I live in Denver now, but I was born right here in Whitchee Twitchee. This place used to be pretty prosperous, but I-75 went West and I-4 went North. That meant Whitchee Twitchee went South. Because it's hard to spell, most folks refer to Whitchee Twitchee, Florida, by its initials, W - T - F.

(MIMI enters.)

COLBY. My Grandma Mimi thinks that's wrong 'cause she says W - T - F means something else ...

MIMI. Well, that's fantastic!

COLBY. Here's a text I got from Grandma today.

MIMI. Heard you're coming to town, Colby. W - T- F !

COLBY. Growing up, my favorite place was Grandma's. She taught me to fish, make sling shots, play a mean game of Texas Hold 'Em, and stand up for myself and anybody—

MIMI. *(To audience.)* –who's getting beat with the short end of a stick by a pole cat!

(MIMI gets a pitcher of Margarita mix and puts it on the table with glasses as COLBY speaks.)

COLBY. Grandma wasn't always like that. Something happened when I was about eight. Me and Mom already moved but I visited Grandma every summer until I discovered football and girls. After high school, I pieced together how and why Grandma changed. Some stuff I picked up *(cont'd)* from newspapers, official records and such, but most came from what I wasn't supposed to hear when I was a little pitcher with big ears.

(CORALEE, wearing what is obviously a wig, and BOBBI enter and greet each other as COLBY moves to his prop area, still speaking.)

COLBY. Grown-ups think kids aren't paying attention. Oh, they are. One thing I can guarantee, if it went down the way I think it did, Grandma had help. See, my Grandma and her best friends…Miss Bobbi...and Miss Coralee...met every Friday and played poker for quarters. Their card club was mostly an excuse to talk about important things, like should city hall put petunias or geraniums in the window boxes? Or will the Dolphins *(you can insert your local losing sports team here and in every reference to the Dolphins.)* be in the basement, again? And they'd solve problems while they played. Their problems, yours, anybody's, whether you wanted them to or not.

CORALEE. Good as Dr Phil or Dr. Ruth!

MIMI. Better! We've been doing it a long time, too. Bobbi, tell how we got together.

BOBBI. Well, we've known each other since grade school and who knows, maybe there was something in the water? We all had baby girls around the same time and we ended up raising them by ourselves. That was something special we had in common *(To CORALEE)* besides being stuck the same small town with certain people who desperately need a make-over.

CORALEE. And who made you the WTF Fashion Police! Just because you worked at Dress Barn one Christmas does not make you an expert on what to wear.

(MIMI hands them their drinks.)

MIMI. Coralee! Bobbi! Stop it!

BOBBI. I'm sorry, Coralee. Now go ahead and I promise I won't say a word about that sad-ass wig you're wearing.

CORALEE. Well, soon as I got my first job, I got a car. Then I had two accidents. One tore off a fender, the other showed up 9 months later. I named my daughter Junelee.

MIMI. My husband, Bill, was a lineman for the phone company. When our Lisa was two, he fell off a bucket truck, bounced three times, and beamed straight to heaven, which he would want me to say...because he loved Star Trek.

BOBBI. Please. Don't tell these nice people who-all my ex was sleeping with!

CORALEE. Who wasn't Richard sleeping with?

MIMI. Besides us?

BOBBI. I swear. That man had more side dishes than the deli at Piggly Wiggly. After the divorce, I raised my daughter, Amy, with no help at all from her dad.

CORALEE. Amy. What a sweetheart. I always thought she'd be a nurse. Remember when she was little? She'd always be carrying around a shoe box with a broken-wing bird, or a bent-tail mouse.

BOBBI. Amy was like that. If something was damaged, she was set on saving it, for better or worse.

MIMI. We tried to keep Amy and all our children safe and keep each other from falling apart. We raised those girls together, from binkies to Barbies, to the birds and the bees. And in a small town, there is a lot of pollinating to nip in the bud!

BOBBI. And remember when you got the big C, Coralee?

CORALEE. How could I forget? You tag teamed, driving me to treatments, and made me laugh going and coming. That was truly special.

BOBBI. You know what else was special? The time we murdered all those men.

MIMI. Bobbi! Shh!! That was pure-D self-defense. I realize a court didn't say that, but trials are expensive. We saved the county a ton!

CORALEE. But we could have been in "People Magazine" and famous.

MIMI. Famous as in "Look What Florida Man's Grandmother done did."

COLBY. Bobbi, Coralee, and Grandma Mimi are leaving out a lot. It's understandable, up to a point. Routine life in WTF dragged on for years. It wasn't unusual when Coralee's daughter and my mom moved away. Most of the young people around here did. So, it was surprising, and happy for Bobbi, her Amy stayed. She married a local boy who inherited his dad's insurance agency. He swept Amy off her feet and tolerated Bobbi.

Life was pretty good for Bobbi until something terrible happened. One day, Amy went to the mailbox and a car nobody saw hit the mailbox, and Amy. Amy's death shook everybody bad. Grandma and Coralee had a heck of a time getting Bobbi through something you never get over. Eventually with tears, tissues, pie, poker, and a trip to the beauty parlor, Bobbi started easing back to life. Then, *(JIM enters)* Bobbi's son-in--law, Jim, asked Bobbi to meet him at his office.

(JIM sits at his desk, engrossed in paperwork. BOBBI moves to Jim's Office with a casserole dish. COLBY watches her from his corner, as do MIMI and CORALEE as they sit at Mimi's table.)

JIM. Hello, Bobbi. Have a seat.

BOBBI. Thanks. And this is for you. It's my green bean casserole, the one you like with the cream of mushroom soup and the crunchy onion rings on top.

JIM. If it's not hot, you can put it on the desk. Otherwise, set it on the floor.

BOBBI. Are you OK?

JIM. I'm OK.

BOBBI. In case you're wondering about me, I truly am sorry I haven't called since the funeral. I hope you'll forgive me.

JIM. No need for that, but I do need to talk to you.

BOBBI. First, I want you to know, I will always consider you family. It's just until last week, I couldn't make myself get out of the house.

JIM. Well, it's good to hear you can get out of the house because, you've got to get out of the house.

BOBBI. Excuse me?

JIM. Here. Remember this?

BOBBI. Sure. That's the quit claim deed to my house I signed for Amy, so she didn't have to go through probate. We agreed she'd file it when I passed.

JIM. Right. And you realize I'm her executor and heir.

BOBBI. OK.

JIM. The deed passes to me.

BOBBI. I have no problem with that.

JIM. You don't understand. I'm filing it this Monday. You've got to the end of the month then I'm listing the house for sale.

BOBBI. What?

JIM. You heard me.

BOBBI. I heard you, but this is where you say, "Gottcha. Just joking!" You are joking...aren't you?

JIM. No, I'm not. There's boxes in the back. Take what you need.

BOBBI. Boxes? Are you serious? Did you just tell me you want to take my house and now, you're doing me a favor giving me cardboard boxes? How about I do you a favor and take you to the hospital because you are crazy!

JIM. Don't get dramatic.

BOBBI. I'll get in whatever state I want. I paid off that place cleaning houses and driving school buses with no air conditioning while I raised Amy and you expect me to say, "Fine?"

JIM. Yeah. And when this is over, you and me, we're done.

BOBBI. Wait a minute! I don't think you can do this. And if you could, why? Doesn't make sense. By God, I am not leaving my house!

JIM. OK.

BOBBI. OK? Seriously?

JIM. Sure. You don't have to move.

BOBBI. Thank God!

JIM. I'll sell the house back to you.

BOBBI. What?

JIM. Two hundred thousand *(or whatever amount is the going rate for a modest rural house in your area. Change the amount consistently within the script.)* and I tear this up.

BOBBI. You want two hundred thousand dollars? You got Amy's life insurance. I'm glad to give you the house when I'm gone, but if you think I've got that kind of money, you swallowed a stupid stick. I got no place to go. It's not right and—

JIM. What's not right about what's legal? This is business, Bobbi. After the court enters the deed, I want a set of keys. Oh, and by the way. I hate this gooey crap.

(JIM dumps the casserole in a trash can beside his desk. BOBBI is nothing to him and she feels that way. As BOBBI gets up and walks back to take a seat at Mimi's table, COLBY speaks.)

COLBY. After Bobbi stopped crying long enough to drive and make some phone calls, she headed to Grandma's to tell her and Coralee what happened.

(JIM sits quietly as BOBBI joins MIMI and CORALEE at the table.)

BOBBI. And then he said, "By the way, I hate this gooey crap," and threw my casserole in the trash.

MIMI. Well! That dills my pickle.

CORALEE. Hell. Dill his pickle.

MIMI. Oh, Bobbi, you can stay with me if you if you need to.

BOBBI. Thank you. I just can't believe Jim's gone so low.

MIMI. Lower than a snake in a sewer. Did you call a lawyer?

BOBBI. Yes. They said I should have called before I gave Amy a quit claim deed from cheap legal forms dot com.

CORALEE. Don't you blame yourself for a second. You were just trying to make things easier for Amy.

BOBBI. I never thought my baby would go before me.

MIMI. Nobody thinks that. You couldn't have known. And who would have guessed Amy married a Klingon.

BOBBI. Snidely Whiplash--

CORALEE. Dr Jekyll and Mr. Jerk-aw--

MIMI. Coralee!

BOBBI. Well, she's right.

CORALEE. Girls, this is terrible. We've got to fix this, together!

(CORALEE stands holding an imaginary sword aloft.)

All for one and one for all, just like the three Mouseketeers!!

(MIMI and BOBBI look at CORALEE, then at each other.)

CORALEE. What?!

MIMI. Musk-keteers, Coralee, not Mouse-keteers.

BOBBI. Oh, don't you never mind. Right now, I'd be thrilled if the three Stooges saved me.

MIMI. Well, obviously, Jim is messed up as a kite in a hailstorm. Here you are, still grieving your daughter! *(CORALEE sits; MIMI stands)* And he puts you through this? Well, when somebody's ugly to people I love, it burns my gravy something fierce!...I'm going to have a talk with him.

CORALEE. Would you?

BOBBI. Really?

MIMI. Sure will. Other than wasting my breath, can't hurt.

(JIM silently begins a call as MIMI walks to Jim's Office.)

COLBY. Grandma worried all night about what to say to Jim. Normally, she was so nice you'd think she was Canadian. It wasn't her nature to call people out, but Mimi had calculated her closet space. If Bobbi moved in, there'd only be room for half her shoes. So, the next morning, Grandma headed to the Orange Blossom Insurance Agency to convince Jim of the errors of his ways.

(COLBY exits. JIM speaks pleasantly on the phone as MIMI enters and listens unseen by JIM.)

JIM. Yes, I'll have that policy to you first thing Tuesday. I'll email the invoice...You're more than welcome...You have a great weekend yourself, Mrs. Dahl, and thanks for your business. *(Hangs up.)* Old prune.

(MIMI steps into Jim's line of sight.)

MIMI. Hello, Jim.

JIM. *(Flatly)* Oh. Hi, Mimi. I'm getting ready to close for the day. My girl's gone until Monday. Call then and make an appointment with her.

MIMI. Well, I just need to talk to you about one little thing and it won't take long. It would mean a lot to me and--

JIM. I just have a second. Is this about a new policy?

MIMI. No. Listen. I know you've probably done some really nice things in your life, but lately? You've been selfish and, well, downright mean!

JIM. Pardon?

MIMI. You have done a bad, bad thing to Bobbi.

JIM. I don't know what you're talking about.

MIMI. Oh, yes, you do.

JIM. Mimi, I do not have time right now for this, or you. I've got to go.

MIMI. Sit down. We are not done here, young man. You are trying to put Bobbi on the street. Shame on you! You're her son-in-law.

JIM. Exactly. That's why this is between me and her. It's not your business. Besides, you have no idea. Bobbi's a snob, a, a terrible cook, and she was a lousy mother-in-law.

MIMI. So? A mother-in-law is supposed to be lousy! That changes nothing. Now, give me the deed to Bobbi's house.

JIM. You need to leave right now. I'm calling the police.

MIMI. You go ahead and call but if I leave without that deed, I'm calling the newspaper. They'll interview me and everybody will know what you're doing to Bobbi! No, I won't. Takes too long. I'm putting this on Facebook! And I may even learn to Tweet!

JIM. Hold on! You're talking blackmail. Ruin my business and I'll sue. You want to lose your house, too?

MIMI. You just worry about yourself, mister. You can become a very determined person when Father Time is breathing down your neck. And right now, he's so close I can smell what he had for lunch.

JIM. ... Huh. You know what, Mimi? I hate to admit this. It's hard to say, but you're right. I guess I haven't been myself since, well, you know. The fact is, Bobbi should stay in that house as long as she wants. Can you forgive me?

MIMI. ...Well! Really? OK. Sure. And thank you. Amy would be happy you're doing the right thing.

JIM. And I am. Come on. Let's drive to my place and get the deed.

MIMI. Wait a minute! Bobbi said it's in your desk.

JIM. Give me a break, OK? Seriously, I hardly know what day it is since Amy died. I'll check. It's probably right here...

(JIM pulls out a gun and aims it at MIMI.)

Yep. This is what I'm looking for.

MIMI. Oh Lord. No! No, Jim. Don't do this. Aww! Nooo!

JIM. Hands up, Mimi.

MIMI. Listen, you shoot me, and your life will be so messed up nobody can fix it. And I am not ready to die! But I was looking forward to my life flashing in front of me. There was that first kiss in 8th grade under the bleachers with Doug Barnes and--

JIM. Shut up! Just shut up! Here's what's gonna happen. Folks will think you wandered off, until they find you and your car at the bottom of the swamp. Or maybe they won't find you, ever. Now put your hands up and don't move.

(JIM picks up his cell phone from the desk and dials it trying to keep the gun on MIMI .)

JIM. Yeah, it's me...Yeah. Can you meet me at the Caloosahatchee bridge in half an hour?...Important? If you want your money, yeah, I'd say it's important. I just need a ride back to town...Alright…Bye.

(As JIM moves his gun hand to the phone to end the conversation, MIMI lurches forward fast, grabs his arm with the gun, and turns away from the audience with JIM behind her facing the same way. They struggle then the gun fires. SFX: BANG! MIMI turns and checks herself while JIM stiffens in pain.)

MIMI. Am I dead?

JIM. That was stupid. Now turn around.

(JIM is the one who turns, holding onto the desk. JIM plops in his chair, flops across the desk face first and opens a squib attached to his chest so "blood" seeps through. JIM lets both arms droop over his head, drops the gun on the desk, and is still.)

MIMI. Oh, Mimi. What have you done?? Ohhhh! Ohhhhh!

(MIMI gingerly pulls turns JIM's head to see it better, then she lets it flop down. MIMI picks up JIM's downstage arm by the wrist and flaps his hand up and down then lets it drop.)

MIMI. Ohhhh, Lord! Help!

(An anxious MIMI talks to herself as COLBY enters. While COLBY speaks, MIMI regains her gumption.)

COLBY. Grandma Mimi admitted she made a lot of mistakes in her life, but she was a practical, positive person who believed things generally turned out for the best. It was starting to dawn on her, Jim got what he deserved and Grandma being alive was definitely for the best.

MIMI. Bless your heart. I did not mean for you to die. But what's done is done. Besides, you wanted to kill me! I just wanted to talk. I tell you what, if there is an after-life, I hope Amy is kicking your ass right now for screwing over her mother.

(MIMI makes a call to Coralee. CORALEE picks up the phone.)

CORALEE. Hello.

MIMI. Coralee, it's me.

CORALEE. *(To BOBBI)* It's Mimi. *(TO MIMI)* You OK?

MIMI. Yes, I'm OK but ah--

BOBBI. Put her on speaker. Is she OK?

(CORALEE puts phone on table between her and BOBBI.)

CORALEE. What do you mean OK but?

MIMI. I'm OK but get yourselves over here. Things got a little caddy-wonked.

CORALEE. Why? That no-good sack of pig slime won't cooperate?

MIMI. Well, not exactly. It's, it's gone way beyond that.

BOBBI. What do you mean?

MIMI. Well, he's kind of, sort of, dead.

CORALEE. Mimi, Jim can't be kinda sorta dead. He's either dead or he's not.

MIMI. Well, if you put it that way, he's dead. I'll explain later. Throw some cleaning supplies in the car and get over here, quick!

(BOBBI and CORALEE move to Jim's Office as COLBY speaks and MIMI waits.)

COLBY. Coralee and Bobbi high-tailed it fast as they could without triggering the speed trap on US 27. Grandma needed them and they needed to figure out what happened.

MIMI. Thank you for coming so fast.

BOBBI. He really is dead!

MIMI. He sure ain't playing possum.

CORALEE. I've never seen anybody fresh dead before, except from natural causes.

MIMI. Well, the bullet went into his chest, and naturally, he died.

BOBBI. You shot him?

MIMI. No! He shot himself with this.

(MIMI picks up the gun on the desk. As she talks, she gestures wildly with it while BOBBI and CORALEE weave and duck.)

CORALEE. He committed suicide?

MIMI. No! I told him I wanted the deed and he pulled this gun on me and then he made a call about meeting somebody after pushing me and my car in the river. I figured I had nothing to lose so I grabbed the gun or one second more, I'd be sleeping with the crawfish.

BOBBI. I didn't even know he owned gun.

CORALEE. Hello! This is Florida. <u>Everybody</u> owns a gun.

(MIMI puts the gun in the back of her pants.)

BOBBI. We better call the police.

CORALEE. Uh, uh! Don't you watch "Law and Order?" *(Or any popular crime solving show.)* Mimi was trying to get the deed to your house.

BOBBI. So? We're senior citizens. We can get away with anything. Can't we?

CORALEE. Jim's secretary knows you were here yesterday, right?

BOBBI. Oh, I forgot about that.

CORALEE. And Mimi, if they find one little fingerprint and the police find out you and Bobbi are in cahoots, which you are, everything goes to Jim's family. How can you prove who shot who?

BOBBI. Oh, Lord, this is all my fault. *(To MIMI)* I almost got you killed, my son-in-law is dead, I'm going to jail, and I'm pretty sure I can't take my CPAP machine.

MIMI. You know what? I hate to say this, but if nobody finds the deed, or the body, he's just a missing person, no different than what he planned for me. Maybe folks will just think he couldn't handle living here without Amy.

(MIMI pokes JIM in the back.)

BOBBI. Jim was a terrible person, but I did not want him dead, at least not in his office. Coralee, what does "where to hide a body dot com" say?

(CORALEE consults her cell phone.)

CORALEE. Swamps are better. Darn, we can't take him there tonight.

BOBBI. Why?

CORALEE. None of us can drive after dark.

MIMI. Shoot! He's as much trouble dead as he was alive. So, what are we going to do with him?

(MIMI puts a hand on JIM's back and rests her weight on it like JIM's a piece of furniture while she thinks. BOBBI pipes up.)

BOBBI. How about your deep freeze? At least 'til we think of something better.

MIMI. I suppose. I don't think anybody will look for him at my house.

CORALEE. Good thinking. Let's sit him up.

(CORALEE stands behind Jim's chair and motions MIMI and BOBBI to get on either side of her behind the chair.)

Come on. We'll roll him out back and put him in my trunk.

(CORALEE grabs JIM under his arms. BOBBI and MIMI grab hold of either side of his chest and a shoulder.)

CORALEE. Ready? Three, two, one lift!

(The WOMEN grunt and gasp as they heave-ho like pirates lifting a treasure chest. With a mighty last effort on "lift," JIM sits with his arms straight up and head flopped down. The WOMEN are on the same page as THEY team up and try different things—like bending JIM's hands, karate chopping at his elbows, slapping him on the head with his own hands, doing a "wave" with his arms—to get his arms in his lap.)

MIMI. I'll need to lock up the office. Now, where are his keys?

BOBBI. Probably in his pants.

MIMI. Oh, yuck.

(MIMI bends over beside JIM, puts a hand in his front pant pocket, and cautiously feels around.)

MIMI. Nothing!

CORALEE. *(To BOBBI)* Check the other side.

(BOBBI reaches into his other pant pocket and feels around. MIMI decides to try again, too. Then, they are both reaching in his pants while rhythmically moving up and down together. JIM seems to be enjoying the attention and moans suggestively. MIMI, CORALEE and BOBBI screech and jump back away from him and group together. JIM groans, gasps, looks down at his chest at the blood stain.)

JIM. What the?...Oww!... Blood? On my brand-new shirt? Ohhh! Now I remember. Damn you, Mimi! You shot me!

MIMI. I did not! You shot yourself. If I shot you, you'd be dead.

JIM. *(To BOBBI)* And you! I should have known you were behind this. You are in so much trouble, you have no idea. I can't wait to throw you out *(JIM stands*) just like that disgusting green bean casserole. And you know what? I think that's the last thing Amy ate before she died. Yeah, she was probably dizzy with food poisoning and didn't see the car. Ow. Damn! This hurts, bad!

(JIM falls back in his chair again.)

Bobbi, call 911. I need an ambulance, now!

BOBBI. If you say you're sorry! Say it!

JIM. I am. So, so sorry. Sorry Mimi didn't take that bullet.

(MIMI raises her arm fast and aims the gun at JIM with determination. He gets up and leans on the desk.)

JIM. Put that down. You know you can't do it.

(MIMI holds firm, then hesitates and starts to lower her arm.)

MIMI. Oh, Spit! I can't!

(JIM turns towards MIMI to grab the gun, but BOBBI grabs MIMI's hand holding the gun, raises MIMI's arm and shoots. SFX BANG!)

JIM. Not again. Did you really think that would w--

(JIM staggers back, slumps in his chair and shuts down. After a beat, CORALEE walks over and pokes JIM to see if he reacts.)

CORALEE. Just in case, you want me to sit on him?

BOBBI. I'm pretty sure I got him, but you know what? I almost felt sorry for him, but *(To MIMI)* I could <u>never</u> give him another chance to hurt you!

CORALEE. *(To BOBBI)* And don't forget, he attacked your cooking.

MIMI. If it makes any difference, Bobbi, I love your casserole.

CORALEE. Well, you won't get any in jail.

BOBBI. Oh, Lord! Jail!

(BOBBI holds on to Jim's desk, lowers herself to her knees, and prays.)

Lord, when I go to jail, please, put Mimi and Coralee in my cell. And may I get the bottom bunk, amen.

CORALEE. Seriously? You want all this on top?...

(BOBBI gets back up as MIMI speaks.)

MIMI. Would you two stop pecking at each other? We don't have time. Get him out the back door, load him up and get him to my place. I'll clean like Martha Stewart's coming to town and meet you later. Hurry, hurry, hustle! Take the gun, and the deed, and, yep, grab that cell phone. Go! Git!!

(Comical fast MUSIC plays. BOBBI helps CORALEE roll JIM out as MIMI shoos them offstage.)

TO BLACK:

END OF ACT ONE, SCENE 1.

ACT ONE

SCENE 2

Setting: The Auto Body Shop, formerly Jim's Office, is dark. The desk is pushed back. There's a "Bump and Grind Auto Shop" sign and pin ups that occasionally catch STAN's attention later in this scene. Mimi's kitchen is also dark.

At Rise: MUSIC fades down. THUNDER SFX up and STROBE effect on dark stage. CORALEE, MIMI, & BOBBI enter. They are wearing black garbage bag ponchos, colorful dish-washing gloves, shower caps, goggles and snorkel masks, while carrying body parts wrapped in freezer paper. The lights fade up to reveal the women standing in a line, their backs to the audience.

(The WOMEN turn and face the audience. They are still until any audience reaction fades. MIMI goes to the freezer, opens the lid, dumps her package inside, and motions the others to dump theirs in. They ceremoniously do so. CORALEE and BOBBI head to the Kitchen Table. MIMI gently closes the freezer and returns to the table where CORALEE and BOBBI are taking off their gloves, eye wear and caps. MIMI does, too.)

BOBBI. Dang! I lost a nail.

CORALEE. I could use a drink.

MIMI. Me, too. I'm nervous as a long-tailed cat in a room full of rocking chairs.

BOBBI. Count me in.

MIMI. I've got something that'll hit the spot. I'll be right back.

(MIMI gets tequila and shot glasses on a tray.)

BOBBI. Coralee! Where'd you learn to do that?

CORALEE. What?

BOBBI. What you just did in the garage.

CORALEE. Oh! Before "The *(Golden)* Bachelor," my favorite show was "Dexter." *(Insert current shows featuring romance and grisly murders if those mentioned are passe.)*

MIMI. OK, girls. This should take the edge off. Here, one for you, and you, and me! I propose a toast.

BOBBI. My son-in-law's in your freezer. What's there to toast?

MIMI. You! Living peacefully in your house, as long as you want.

BOBBI. That is wonderful. Thank you both! Cheers, dears.

(THEY drink.)

MIMI. No reason to stop at one. Who wants a refill?

CORALEE. Me-eee!

BOBBI. Me, too.

(MIMI pours another round. THEY toast each other and down the shot.)

MIMI. It's strange, but I'm not feeling as bad about all this as I thought I would.

CORALEE. You just had two shots of 80 proof tequila, and you didn't really kill Jim.

MIMI. But I thought I did.

BOBBI. Mimi, he was going to feed you to the gators.

CORALEE. *(To BOBBI)* And make you a bag lady.

BOBBI. Pour another!

(MIMI obliges)

I have a toast. To Mimi! The best-est and bravest friend a girl could ever have.

MIMI. Aww. You're going to make me cry.

CORALEE. Before you start, what are we going to do with you-know-who?

MIMI. I don't know. We'll figure it out when folks forget about him in a couple weeks. Besides, don't matter if he gets freezer burn. It's not like he's pecans, or wedding cake.

BOBBI. You have the deed?

MIMI. Yep. Here it is. It's all yours Bobbi. If I were you, I'd tear that into tiny pieces and burn it. Ready for another?

(MIMI pours)

BOBBI. Okey dokey! And here's another toast. To not sleeping in my car!

CORALEE And no bird baths in the "Wawa" *(insert your local gas/convenient store chain*) rest room.

BOBBI. No fights over the bottom bunk.

CORALEE. No listening to you snore.

MIMI. And since Sherlock Holmes ain't real, nobody will ever have a clue what happened today. Salud, y'all.

(EVERYONE smiles and toasts. As THEY start to drink, the freezer lid pops up and a LIGHT glows upward from within. CORALEE does a

spit take. MIMI strides over quickly, slams the lid and gives her friends a reassuring nod, but they put down their glasses, grab their gloves, etc., and exit as fast as they can. COLBY enters and MIMI exits. RANDY, dressed in denim, a Stetson hat and cowboy boots walks out. His cellphone RINGS. He answers it.)

RANDY. Detective Randall McLemore at your service.

(RANDY freezes in place as Colby speaks)

COLBY. Grandma got just one tiny, little, important detail wrong. Sherlock was imaginary but the county just hired its first real detective with a community college degree in criminal justice and 30 years of experience in Uncertain, Texas, where single handed, he sniffed out, literally, a gang that smuggled and sold illegal Mexican purses, made from armadillos.

(As COLBY talks, he pulls glasses and a feathered pen out of his pocket or a prop area within reach and may slap on a woman's wig. He becomes the RECEPTIONIST on the phone with Randy.)

The man was a human bloodhound! And the week after Jim fell off the radar, the Detective got a call.

RANDY. *(Unfreezes)* Just slow down...That's good. Now, take a deep breath. It'll help. Breathe with me

(RANDY takes a deep breath or two to encourage RECEPTIONIST to do the same.)

RECEPT. *(Takes a huge, noisy breath)* Sorry. I get nervous talking to anybody in authority. This is Lucille Roark, Jim McCausey's secretary at the Orange Blossom Insurance Agency.

RANDY. Yes Ma'am. What's wrong? I mean, I figure something's wrong. Nobody calls to say they've made me a mess 'a cookies.

RECEPT. Well, Jim didn't show up for work this week and--

RANDY. Just a sec.

(RANDY watches an insect BUZZING around his head. His hand shoots out fast as a ninja's. RANDY throws the bug down, grinds it under his boot heel and resumes his call.)

RANDY. Go ahead.

RECEPT. As I was saying, Jim didn't show up for work Monday or Tuesday or Wednesday or --

RANDY. --Maybe he's sick or having fun. Maybe there's a family emergency. We can't say a grown man's missing because he's gone a couple days.

RECEPT. But he was supposed to go to the courthouse Monday for something. He didn't, his car's in the lot, he's not answering his phone or emails, and he's not at home. I checked. Knocked on all the windows and doors, not a peep from anybody, and he always lets me know if he's going away.

RANDY. When did you see him last?

RECEPT. Friday. Saturday morning, he comes in by his-self.

RANDY. Was he married? Single? Divorced?

RECEPT. Actually, his wife died in February. Remember that hit and run?

RANDY. I wasn't working here then so, no. Does he have other family 'round here?

RECEPT. His mother-in-law, Amy's mom, Bobbi. Come to think of it, she came by Friday. Had an appointment, what for I don't know.

RANDY. Text me her contact info, and your boss's. I'll go by his place, stop at yours, then visit Ms. Bobbi. And don't you worry. I always get my armadillo. *(Winces)* I mean man.

RECEPT. Well, it could be a gal. Women can snap.

RANDY. True, but I'm sure not you. Such an, interesting, voice. You know, ah, since I'm new to these parts, I wonder, can you tell me where a widower, like me, might go to meet a respectable lady who might—

RECEPT. --Might what? Might cook? Might clean and take care of him while her youth fades? Then *(Snobs, sniffles)* he bails for a blonde with store bought headlights who works at a club in Orlando?

RANDY. Sorry for your loss. I didn't mean nothin'. And I'll find your boss! See you later. *(Hangs up.)* Doggone it!

(RANDY slumps off. COLBY speaks as he puts away the RECEPTIONIST costume elements, picks up a black hat, and hides a roll of toilet paper under his arm. He is becoming HARRY.)

COLBY. Meanwhile, on the other side of the tracks, Harry, owner of the Bump and Grind auto body shop, called his ever so faith-less employee, Stan. Harry didn't know it yet, but he and Detective Randy had a lot in common. They were both looking for Jim.

(After his last line as COLBY, HARRY sits, glares towards the audience, and makes a call on his cell phone.)

HARRY. Come on Stan. Where the hell are you?

(STAN, in a work shirt, backwards ball cap, and a blacked out front tooth, walks out carrying a shop broom. He ogles the pin-ups as he enters, then answers the phone with his free hand.)

STAN. Bump and Grind Auto Shop. We put the curves back in your car. We make your wheels go wheeee again! Bring us your dents, you won't repent--

HARRY. --Shut up, Stan! It's me. Don't you look at caller ID?

STAN. *(Defensively)* Just practicing our motto like you told me. *(Seriously)* Did you find Jim?

HARRY. No, I'm at his office now and--

STAN. Ain't it kinda stupid showing up where he works?

HARRY. I didn't walk in and say, "Hi, there. I'm Jim's friendly neighborhood loan officer. Where's the best place to corner the creep?"

STAN. Well, what did you say?

HARRY. I asked to use the restroom.

STAN. OK. What did you find out?

(HARRY holds up the toilet paper admiringly and rubs it on his cheek.)

HARRY. That this place has the softest toilet paper! But no Jim. He wasn't at the bridge, he ain't here, but his car's in the lot. He ain't returning calls or texts. He's making me feel like a one-night stand.

STAN. That's a pretty good sign Jim's skipped town. Or he's not goin' out with <u>you</u> again.

(STAN guffaws at his own remark. An irate HARRY glares.)

HARRY. Stan, practice this motto. "Nobody likes a smart ass!" It is hard to believe there's anybody more annoying than you but Jim ain't put his mother-in-law's house up for sale so we can settle up. I tell you what, if I cain't get it from him, I'm gonna get my money from the old broad. Everybody always pays Harry Blevins, with interest.

STAN. What you gonna do if she doesn't cooperate?

HARRY. What do you think?

(HARRY pulls an imaginary handle on his chair. We hear a toilet FLUSH SFX. HARRY gets up, takes off his hat and speaks as COLBY.)

COLBY. Harry was the rotten apple at the bottom of Jim's barrel, but Grandma didn't know that yet. So, for a couple days, she and her friends concentrated on enjoying life and each other. That didn't last long.

(COLBY exits and BOBBI and CORALEE enter. We hear NATURE SFX. CORALEE has branch pruners and BOBBI has a rake. They work" while they talk.)

BOBBI. Thanks for coming over to help, Coralee

(NATURE SFX fade down)

CORALEE. Glad to. Pruning is good for the bust line. Last time I went to Beall's *(insert your local department store with women's clothing.)* for a blouse the clerk sent me to the Sag Harbor section. Who thought that was a good name for women's clothes? *(Looks down at her chest.)* Sag Harbor. No <u>man</u> would ever buy shorts labeled Limp Lagoon. Anyway, I always feel happy working outside.

BOBBI. Here we are getting blisters and you're cheerful.

CORALEE. Not all the time. I've got my moments. No sex in 7 years wears on you.

BOBBI. So you and that UPS driver <u>did</u> have a fling!

CORALEE. Not for long. He asked annoying questions. "What's for breakfast?" "What's for lunch?" "How much do you weigh?" Men want me to cook, but they don't want me to eat.

BOBBI. If you're lonesome, why don't you get out where you can meet a man? You've got a wonderful voice! Go to one of those Karaoke places in a big city like Arcadia. *(Insert a your town or one nearby town or area folks joke about.)*

CORALEE. Naw. My dating pool's the dead sea. The only single man I know is in Mimi's freezer.

(Spaghetti western MUSIC that only CORALEE hears catches CORALEE's attention. She looks off in the distance and alerts BOBBI. MUSIC fades down.)

CORALEE. Bobbi! Looky, look, look what's coming.

(*CORALEE and BOBBI watch RANDY saunter onstage. CORALEE is gob smacked.)*

RANDY. Howdy, ladies. (*RANDY tips his hat to them.)* Good morning. Hope I'm not interrupting. Name's Randall McLemore. Detective Randall McLemore.

(CORALEE sidles in front of BOBBI to greet RANDY first.)

CORALEE. It is a pleasure! Sorry. I am Coralee Campbell. And this is Bobbi Rose.

RANDY. Nice to meet you ladies. And would you look at Bobbi Rose's beautiful roses!

(RANDY squats as if to smell one and picks up some "dirt," speaking as he gets up.)

What kind of fertilizer do you use?

BOBBI. Blood meal.

(CORALEE elbows BOBBI disapprovingly.)

RANDY. You don't say. *(Smells dirt in his hand.)* Yep. Ace Hardware brand. *(RANDY throws dirt down.)*

BOBBI. Yes, but, how did—

RANDY. —I'll have to try that. I like flowers. Nice day, too. Oh, I almost forgot. Ms. Bobbi, did you know your son-in-law Jim is missing?

BOBBI. Jim? Missing? My goodness. Coralee, did you know Jim's missing?

CORALEE. How would I know your son-in-law is missing if you don't know he's missing?

RANDY. Well, then I'm sorry to be the one to have to tell you, but nobody's heard hide nor hair from him. Do you remember how he was feeling, or what he had to say last time you saw him?

BOBBI. Oh, gosh, that was a while back. He was married to my daughter who passed. Amy.

RANDY. *(Takes off his hat respectfully.)* I heard about your loss and I'm truly sorry. I also heard from his office gal you met Jim last Friday before he dropped off the radar so to speak. *(Puts his hat back on.)*

BOBBI. Oh, my. Ah, you're right. I forgot. Death affects your memory. Any death.

RANDY. Yes, Ma'am. I understand completely. But now that you remember meeting, maybe you can tell me about it. Could be important. Any detail. I'd appreciate anything.

BOBBI. Well..ah, oh, lemme see, hmm--

CORALEE. Bobbi, what is wrong with you? You said Jim had pictures of you and Amy that he wanted you to have.

BOBBI. Oh, that's right, he did!

RANDY. May I see them?

BOBBI. Well, sure. I think I put them in the house somewhere. I'd have to look.

RANDY. I'll wait. Got nothing else to do and I like being outside. Except when there's bugs.

BOBBI. Oh. OK. *(Turns and then looks back)* Coralee, can you help?

(BOBBI takes her rake and grabs CORALEE's arm.)

CORALEE. OK

(CORALEE smiles at RANDY, takes her pruners and walks with BOBBI. They stack their tools near an exit and conspire. RANDY squats and takes another handful of dirt, shakes it, gets up, looks at his watch, then starts swatting at bugs around his face, looks off in the distance, rub his hands, his chin, polishes his badge--does anything but look at the women.)

BOBBI. What will I do? I don't have any pictures of Amy that aren't framed.

CORALEE. Let's look like we've been searching. Come on!

(CORALEE leads BOBBI in a couple of high knee raises, then jumping jack arms. Finally, CORALEE gets BOBBI to try some belly dance moves to MUSIC before they hobble back, huffing and puffing, to RANDY.)

BOBBI. Whew! I am out of breath, and so sorry. I can't remember where I put that envelope. And that's the truth!

RANDY. Well, I hope you find those precious memories. By the way, I'm looking into re-opening your daughter's hit and run case. And if you think of anything else about Jim that might be helpful, or you hear anything, or you just need something, you call me. Here's my card.

(CORALEE gets in front of BOBBI again and gives RANDY a big smile)

CORALEE. Oh, ah, can I have one, Randall?

RANDY. Certainly**.** My pleasure. And you can me Randy.

CORALEE. Thank you, Sweetie, I mean Randy. Ahem, I mean, Detective. Nice meeting you.

RANDY. *(To BOBBI)* And nice meeting you, too.

(RANDY starts to leave.)

BOBBI. You let us know what you find out, hear?

RANDY. I will, and I'll likely see you ladies soon. I'm new. Not much else to do around here.

(RANDY tips his hat, turns, and exits singing "One way, or another, I'm gonna find ya, I'm gonna get ya get ya get ya" with rhythm in his walk and a little butt action before he disappears off stage.)

CORALEE. He sure is handsome!

BOBBI. He sure is nosy.

CORALEE. That's his job. And I didn't see a wedding ring.

BOBBI. Coralee, what is wrong with you? He's looking for Jim!

CORALEE. He can look all he wants and he's not going to find anything but little old me with a heart big as my butt. Think he's a real cowboy?

(COLBY enters and quietly watches.)

BOBBI. Coralee, you think you're rowing to the Love Boat but you're heading for the Titanic. Snap out of it! We've got to tell Mimi about this.

(BOBBI and CORALEE sit at the Kitchen Table. They start playing cards as COLBY speaks. There is a pie on the table or nearby.)

COLBY. If Randy had been married, Coralee would have been sad as a bird without a tail. But he wasn't, so the timing couldn't be worse. Grandma always said, what's *(cont'd)* meant to be, will be, and there's not a darn thing you can do about it. That's what she says, but this time, she definitely tried to change things for the better.

(MIMI enters, sits and picks up her cards as COLBY exits.)

MIMI. I didn't even know the county had a detective. (*To BOBBI*) I'll see you and raise fifty cents.

BOBBI. He's so new even Coralee didn't know him.

CORALEE. He looks...experienced.

BOBBI. Let's hope experienced doesn't mean smart or lucky. We got too much at stake here.

(MIMI takes out a fat joint. She lights it, takes a slow, big toke and holds it before exhaling.)

CORALEE. Mimi, what are you doing??

MIMI. Well, what does it look like? It's perfectly legal…I don't do this to get high.

(BOBBI and CORALEE give her a "look.")

MIMI. It's <u>medical</u> marijuana. My doctor prescribed it for my ...anxiety.

BOBBI. Did you roll that yourself?

MIMI. No, too much arthritis in my fingers. The kid next door helped.

CORALEE. Great. First murder, now delinquency of a minor.

MIMI. Want some?

CORALEE. Oh, why not? My mind's going a mile a minute.

BOBBI. Pass me one.

(MIMI passes CORALEE one and then BOBBI and gives them a lighter they pass and use to light" the joints. They all take a toke.)

BOBBI. Last night, I had a horrible nightmare. I was wearing Crocs with socks. Eww! *(or socks with sandals if Crocs aren't around anymore.)* Here comes the river card. Boom!

CORALEE. Is it my bet? I bet Randy won't find out a thing except that I am one fine woman. And I fold.

BOBBI. You know, I can't make up my mind if he's smart, or dumb as a doorstop. He found out I talked to Jim, but I think he believed me when I said I couldn't recall seeing Jim last Friday.

MIMI. What did he say when you told him that?

BOBBI. *(Looks at joint suspiciously.)* I don't remember. Does this stuff do that to you, too?

(BOBBI takes a big hit.)

MIMI. Too early to tell.

(BOBBI has a severe coughing fit. She comes up for air and smiles.)

Smooottthh!

MIMI. I'll see your 50 cents.

BOBBI. Lay 'em down.

MIMI. Double dog darn you. Triple aces?

CORALEE. Anyway, something still bothers me.

BOBBI. (*Gathering up her chips*) Me winning again or Detective Howdy?

CORALEE. Oh Lord, yes, he bothers me. But I mean why in the world would Jim need so much money he was going to sell your house?

MIMI. Did he have a girlfriend?

(BOBBI shakes her head "no.")

MIMI. Boyfriend?

BOBBI. *(Giggly)* I don't think so.

CORALEE. Did he like expensive things?

BOBBI. Naw. That new shirt he was all worried about was from "The Dollar Store."

MIMI. Well, what he was doing don't really matter now. Everything will be fine. Just don't make that Randy fella suspicious. Be casual, cool. Don't act guilty of nothin' in front of nobody!

(RANDY walks to the kitchen door and KNOCKS. The WOMEN holler, panic and jump up. CORALEE and BOBBI fan the air and bump into each other while MIMI grabs spray air freshener.)

MIMI. Be right there!

(MIMI sprays around the room, at the audience, and under her armpits as she talks while CORALEE gets rid of the ashtray and the joints.)

I'm getting dressed!

(RANDY KNOCKS again.)

MIMI. Wait! Here I come.

(MIMI waves "calm down" to BOBBI and CORALEE. MIMI opens the door halfway. RANDY stands in the partially open doorway. BOBBI poses awkwardly and CORALEE leans seductively with her back against the freezer when they see Randy. MIMI opens the door fully and addresses RANDY.)

MIMI. Oh. Hello. And to whom do I have the pleasure of speaking?

RANDY. Detective Randall McLemore, Ma'am. Here's my card. Howdy, Bobbi. Coralee.

MIMI. I see you've already met the desperate housewives of WTF. I'm Mimi Dooley.

RANDY. It's a pleasure, Miss Mimi. And, by the way, I smelled what you've been doing 20 feet up the walk.

(MIMI throws a leg up and puts her foot on the door frame to block RANDY from coming in.)

CORALEE. It's OK. She's got a prescription, Randy.

MIMI. It's around here someplace.

RANDY. If Miss Coralee says you've got it, we're good. I'm thinking about getting one myself. These knees ache fierce when rain's coming.

CORALEE. Summertime here, that's every 15 minutes. Mimi! Where are your manners? Invite him in.

MIMI. Oh, of course. OK. Come in. Please.

(MIMI lowers her leg and RANDY steps in fast.)

MIMI. So, how did you find me? And why? The only time the law stops here is for Christmas cookies, but they're all gone. Stop by again in December.

(MIMI tries to steer him back to the door but RANDY pushes past to walk further in. RANDY's got something in a plastic bag.)

RANDY. Cookies? I'll be back for sure. Thanks, but right now, I'm looking for Miss Bobbi.

(BOBBI, high as a kite, flashes him a goofy smile and a peace sign.)

She wasn't home and everybody in town said you're friends so I thought you might know where she is, and Bingo!

BOBBI. *(Singing* B-I-N-G-O, B-I-N-G-O, B-I--

CORALEE. --Bobbi, the man's working.

RANDY. Well, Miss Bobbi, I'm sorry but Coralee's right. And I don't know how to make this any easier, but I went by Jim's office and somebody cleaned the place real good. No fingerprints, coffee stains, hair, but I found a page from his desk calendar with a spot, see here?...Darn, I hate to say it, but it looks like dried blood.

BOBBI. Oh! Well, it's probably ah…

CORALEE. A paper cut. Or a mosquito he smacked!

MIMI. They're horrible this year!

RANDY. I hate skeeters! Anyway, I'll run this by forensics. They'll figure it out. But I need you to prepare yourself, just in case. You've been through a passel of heartbreak, and I bet Jim suffered, too.

BOBBI. You could say that. Thank you, Detective, for thinking of me and keeping me informed and for doing such a good job. You have no idea how upsetting this is.

RANDY. Now remember, if you think of anything, anything else about Jim, you call me. You've got my card.

CORALEE. Wait, wait!

(CORALEE puts a slice of pie on a covered plate or in a plastic container.)

Here's a piece of pie to go. I made it.

RANDY. Then I'm sure going to enjoy this. Whoever you're with is lucky to have such a considerate and sweet lady in their life.

CORALEE. They would be, if there was such a person, which there's not right now.

(RANDY starts to say something to CORALEE but MIMI grabs his arm and pulls him to the door.)

MIMI. You be safe out there, detective!

RANDY. *(Turning back)* Most murders are committed by family and friends so I should be safe from you, for now. Right? *(Laughs)* Bye Mimi, Bobbi, Miss Coralee.

(RANDY exits. MIMI watches to make sure he's leaving and calls out to him.)

MIMI. Y'all come back now, hear?

(MIMI shuts and locks the door and plasters herself against it.)

MIMI. I missed blood on Jim's calendar! What else did I mess up? And the detective already knows we're friends and where I live. I'm starting to think he's no dummy. And you-know-who is in my you-know-what! How long before he figures that out?

BOBBI. Mimi, can I have one of those, you know, to take home? I think I need a prescription.

CORALEE. You still meeting us for our salon appointment tomorrow? That'll relax you.

BOBBI. Wouldn't miss it. Got to look good when I win the church chili cook off Sunday. That reminds me, I need to stop by the store on the way home and get up early to start cooking. I sure hope Randy isn't at the grocery. I'm starting to think he's following me.

CORALEE. I'm leaving, too. I wish Randy would follow me!

MIMI. Watch what you wish for!

BOBBI. I wish for a blue ribbon. And Amy. I miss her every day.

MIMI. We do, too. We sure do. You have a good night, Bobbi. See you tomorrow.

(BOBBI and CORALEE leave. HARRY enters the Auto Shop followed by STAN and his broom. MIMI exits.)

STAN. I don't know, Harry. Old ladies are high maintenance.

HARRY. We ain't gonna maintain this one long. First, I gotta find her, then scare her good. Is this Friday?

STAN. Does a fish swim?

HARRY. Can't you answer a question like a normal person? Fridays, everybody in this dump goes to the grocery. I'm surprised Marvin Mart don't hire a band and charge admission. I'll park in the lot and wait.

STAN. While you're there, pick up some of that nice toilet paper for the shop.

HARRY. Get your own, dammit. I do that, next thing, you'll be asking me to cut your meat.

STAN. I'm getting my back pay when you get the money, right? All two years, three months, and fourteen days?

HARRY. Sure, Stan. Every penny.

STAN. Good! Once I get it, I'll hire a be-u-ti-full gal to cook and clean for me wearing nothing but a smile.

HARRY. Who's naked? You or the girl? If it's you, get that tooth fixed so you don't scare her. Or wrap your head in toilet paper...I'm gone.

(HARRY storms off, laughing at Stan. STAN picks up his broom and sings wordlessly with lalas and hums, the "The Cinderella Waltz" as he takes a few turns with it. STAN stops, dips the broom halfway to the floor, strokes its "hair," then rises and addresses the broom.)

STAN. Oh, Ashley, your hair smells so good, but when you dance, you're stiff!

(STAN makes the broom march away from him in little hops.)

Aw, don't get mad. You can't help it. Come on. Let's make up. How about givin' ol' Stan a kiss?

(STAN closes his eyes, puckers up, brings the broom in for a kiss and smacks himself in the face.)

STAN. Ow! Dang women.

(STAN flips the broom over and pushes it across the floor in front of him, fussing, as he exits. MIMI enters smoking a joint. She is a bit giddy.)

MIMI. This stuff sure does help anxiety. I can't remember what I'm supposed to worry about. I know there's something I need to do. Yep! Clean up. Colby's coming! My Colby.

(MIMI grabs the vacuum by the freezer and plugs it below the freezer cord. It won't start. She kicks it and then realizes what's wrong.)

MIMI. Darn it. Why can't I ever remember that plug's broke?

(MIMI unplugs the freezer cord from the top working outlet and replaces it with the vacuum cord.)

Maybe that geeky kid next door can fix it.

(MIMI pats the freezer, then opens the lid and looks inside.)

Don't you worry. I'll plug you back in later.

(MIMI stands up and then looks back in the freezer.)

You alright in there? *(In a deep voice)* S'awright.

(MIMI giggles, slams the freezer lid, takes another toke, starts the VAC and begins to clean, still smoking. The phone in her pocket RINGS. She's frustrated at the interruption but turns off the VAC and answers the phone, facing the audience.)

MIMI. What is it Coralee? You OK?... No, I don't know how to fix a flat, but I can take you to your house, or to a gas station. What'll it be?...I'm on my way.

(MIMI pinches out her joint, puts it in her cleavage before putting the vac back by the freezer. MIMI turns and looks around the kitchen. Is there something she was supposed to do? MIMI shrugs and leaves. COLBY enters.)

COLBY. Meanwhile, Bobbi was leaving Marvin Mart with her prize-winning chili fixings to go home and dream about getting that blue ribbon.

(COLBY exits and prepares to enter quickly as HARRY. BOBBI enters clutching a grocery bag in one hand and a purse on the same elbow. Just in case she's forgetting something, BOBBI checks her bag one last time with her free hand. HARRY enters with a gun in one hand. He sneaks up behind BOBBI as a suspenseful "STINGER" plays.)

BOBBI. Lemme see, ground meat, beans, onions, tomatoes, chili powder…Jack Daniels. Shoot, I forgot crackers.

(BOBBI starts to turn back to the store. HARRY wraps an arm around her neck and covers her mouth with his hand as BOBBI tries to cry out and struggle.)

HARRY. Shut up and don't say nothin'. Got it?

(BOBBI nods.)

HARRY. Good. Now turn around, real slow like.

(HARRY and BOBBI turn slightly as HARRY drops his hand from BOBBI's mouth and rests it on her shoulder, still holding her close.)

See that black Camaro over there? You're gonna walk toward it, real natural. Get in. Make sure you buckle up. And don't do nothin' stupid.

(BOBBI walks offstage nervously while HARRY looks around before exiting casually a few steps behind BOBBI.)

TO BLACK

End of ACT I

INTERMISSION

ACT II,
SCENE 1

Setting: The next morning at the Auto Shop and Mimi's Kitchen where a laptop computer is nearby.

At Rise: BOBBI is tied to a chair in the Auto Shop. She's got a bandana or stretchy gaiter over her mouth and a bag sits loosely over her head. COLBY enters.

COLBY. Hi! And how was intermission, folks? Lovely! And the toilet paper? Soft?...OK! So, as you remember, Randy is looking for Jim who is chillin' in Grandma's freezer. And Grandma didn't know it yet, but Jim's loan arranger, Harry, kidnapped Bobbi. Poor Harry. Bobbi was missing a fingernail, but she had another deadly weapon. Her mouth.

(COLBY leaves to re-enter as HARRY. We hear creative SNORING SFXs that rise, fall, and stutter for a couple beats as BOBBI's head flops and bobs occasionally. HARRY walks out with a gun in one hand and pulls the

bag off BOBBI's head with the other. HARRY watches BOBBI snore for a second or two then pokes her in the shoulder. BOBBI snores louder. HARRY drops the bag, pulls down the bandanna covering BOBBI's mouth, puts the gun under his arm and claps his hands close to her face like applause. BOBBI, half-asleep, blinks and opens her eyes.)

BOBBI. And I want to thank the cook-off judges for first prize and… (*Looks around)* I'm still here? Oh, shoot.

HARRY. Don't tempt me.

BOBBI. You! You are a mean, mean man. I did not get a wink of decent sleep in this doggone chair.

HARRY. That was to get you in the mood to answer questions, old lady.

BOBBI. Don't you call me old lady.

HARRY. Alright. So, what should I call you? How about lumberjack, 'cause you sure snore like one.

BOBBI. My name is Bobbi Rose. What time is it? I got to get my hair done this afternoon and cook for tomorrow.

HARRY. The only thing you need to be worrying about is what's gonna happen if I don't get what I want.

BOBBI. I don't even know you. What do you want? Chili? You stole me and the fixings. Untie me and take me to the kitchen. You got crackers? *(Looks HARRY up and down.)* Never mind, I see you are one.

HARRY. Alright. Think you're funny, huh? Well, you better get serious. I mean business. Where's your son-in-law, Jim?

BOBBI. Him? Ha! He's my ex-son-in-law because he's dead.

HARRY. Dead? You did it, didn't ya!

(BOBBI clenches her mouth shut.)

HARRY. Oh, you better start working that jaw, old lady. Jim owes me a lot of money. And he was gonna sell your house to get it. What did you find out?

BOBBI. Nothing. And I misspoke. I meant he's dead to me. I don't know where he's at. Find out what? He was selling my house to give you money?

HARRY. Yeah! But there's no proof so maybe the police would like to know what you know about what happened to Jim.

(STAN walks in silently behind HARRY.)

BOBBI. Sure, call the po-lice! And while you're at it, tell them you got me tied up in whatever this place is. And tell that to everybody at the church looking forward to my chili.

STAN. Hey, Harry?

HARRY. (*Startled)* Jeez! You scared the hell out of me. And we're not supposed to use our real names, dipstick.

STAN. Well, you just confirmed it was your real name. Otherwise, she wouldn't a' known. I learned that in the pen.

HARRY. What do ya, want?

STAN. There's a cop outside on the sidewalk. Said he wants to talk to you.

HARRY. What about?

BOBBI. Help me! HELP! HELP!

HARRY. Be quiet!

(HARRY pulls the bandanna back over BOBBI's mouth then speaks to STAN.)

HARRY. Watch her. Close.

(RANDY enters and stands "outside" the Auto Shop, waiting. STAN sits with his face about six inches away from BOBBI who watches

back just as intently. HARRY checks his gun then notices them. STAN looks at HARRY.)

STAN. Is this close enough?

(HARRY looks at them with disgust, puts his gun in his back waistband, and walks out to greet Randy in an overly pleasant manner.)

HARRY. Hi there, Officer. What can I do you for?

RANDY. You Harry? Harry Blevins?

HARRY. I am.

RANDY. Howdy, Detective Randall McLemore. Don't wanna keep you long but I'm hoping you can help with a problem--

HARRY.--With your ve-hi-cle? You have come to the right place!

RANDY. No, nope. My car's fine. I'm looking for information. Do you know an insurance agent in town, Jim McCausey?

HARRY. I do. He brought me a lot of business. Or used to until the county took out that confusin' round-a-bout. Something wrong?

RANDY. He's missing. Can't find him nowhere. I'm wondering if you got any ideas where he might a gone off to.

HARRY. Bet he's in Vero Beach, hitting the bars, chatting up the local wildlife. Ol' Jim lost his wife early this year. If a man's lonely, he ain't gonna find much company around here.

RANDY. Don't I know it. But here's the thing. You're not doing a lot of business with Jim, but his desk calendar, well, it shows he had a call to you on his to-do list just about every day. So, why's that?

HARRY. Oh. Well, see, we're fishing buddies. One day he was here, we got talking about those lures you see on the Sunday morning fishing shows. You know, the kind that glow and wiggle and hypnotize bass for only three easy payments of 19.99? Since then, we been out on Lake Okeechobee a couple times. We was planning another trip.

(STAN walks out with his broom.)

STAN. Hey, Harry.

HARRY. What are you doing here instead of doing what you're supposed to be doing? I'm talking to this nice officer.

STAN. I know. I told you he was here...*(To Randy)* Hey. Again. *(To Harry)* Harry, we got a situation.

HARRY. What? Paint not drying fast enough?

STAN. I'm not painting.

HARRY. It's an expression, lug nut.

STAN. Oh. Well, we got a flood, maybe?

HARRY. If it's a "maybe" flood, it's not an emergency. Now how about you get to tending what you're supposed to be tendin' to.

STAN. Alright. Bye, officer. Bye, Harry. *(Exits)*

HARRY. Don't tell me "Bye." I haven't fired you. Yet.

RANDY. Hey, it's OK. I'm going. But if you see Jim or hear anything, give me a call. I want to know he's OK. That's all. Here's my card.

HARRY. You got it.

(HARRY starts to walk away then turns back.)

Wait a minute. Now that I think about it, Jim said something when we was fishing last time, something about his mother-in-law. What's her name? Ah--

RANDY. Bobbi Rose?

HARRY. Yeah. That's it. Bobbi. He said something about loaning her money. You know those old broads and casinos. She got all wrapped up in the slots at Immokalee *(cont'd)* (*insert your local casino or just end at "slots."*). Jim was starting to think she was gonna stiff him because he got her daughters' life insurance. I mean, he's probably fine. But now that I think about it.

RANDY. I talked to Miss Bobbi. Maybe I should go back. Thanks. Appreciate it.

(RANDY exits as HARRY speaks.)

HARRY. There you go. Glad to. You have a good one officer. Bye, now.

(HARRY goes back inside where STAN is waiting for him beside an antsy, squirmy BOBBI.)

HARRY. What is so damn important you had to interrupt me when I was talking to the po-lice?

STAN. She'll tell you.

BOBBI. Mnnnhhnngggbfffmmmmggtbfffffmmm

HARRY. What?

BOBBI. Mnnnhhnngggbfffmmmmggtbfffffmmm

HARRY. Oh, hell.

(HARRY pulls down the bandanna covering BOBBI's mouth.)

BOBBI Oww! I have to go to the bathroom.

HARRY. Again? I took you last night. You ain't had much to drink.

BOBBI. Having my daughter gave me a fallen bladder. You probably gave your mother one just like it.

HARRY. You leave my mom out of this.

STAN. How is your mom?

HARRY. *(Threatens STAN with the back of his hand.)* Shut-up, Stan!

BOBBI. Is your whole name Stanley?

HARRY. Is yours Robert?

BOBBI. Roberta! And Stanley's a nice name.

STAN. I don't like it. But it's better than my brother's.

BOBBI. What's he called?

STAN. Ollie. My mom liked Laurel and Hardy.

BOBBI. Me, too!

HARRY. Will you please take her to the john so I don't have to listen to either of you! Then tie her back up. Move it!

(STAN unties Bobbi. BOBBI struggles to get up and straighten out.)

STAN. Need a hand?

BOBBI. Why, I believe I do.

STAN. Harry bought us some real soft toilet paper.

(STAN offers BOBBI the crook of his arm and leads her off stage, but not before BOBBI turns her head and sticks her tongue out at HARRY while he makes a phone call. CORALEE and MIMI enter the kitchen where CORALEE is talking on her phone.)

HARRY. Come on Jim. Pick up dammit.

CORALEE. ... Hm um, hm.... huh!...mmmmm. Bye.

(HARRY ends the call and exits.)

MIMI. What?? Anything?

CORALEE. Nadine at Marvin Mart said Bobbi's car was in the lot when she closed up last night and it's still there.

MIMI. Ohhhh! I knew something bad's happened. She never misses a hair appointment.

CORALEE. And Nadine said there's a security camera inside the store and one aimed at the lot. The manager records everything in his office. Maybe we can see what happened.

MIMI. Poor Bobbi. I don't know how, but I have a feeling this has something to do with Jim.

CORALEE. Mimi, be honest. If I was missing, would you try to find me?

MIMI. Of course, I would! You're like a sister to me, Coralee. Maybe better. You don't borrow my clothes. Come to think of it, Bobbi's got my new sundress, and my Talbot *(insert a conservative and stylish brand for mature women that your audience will be familiar with.)* skirt, my Chico's pants and--

CORALEE. --Do you want your clothes or Bobbi?

MIMI. Both!

CORALEE. Then, watch out Marvin Mart.

MIMI. Here we come!

(Action MUSIC plays as MIMI and CORALEE put on sunglasses. MIMI waves CORALEE through the door first. MIMI turns around and leans back in, scanning the room before closing the door behind her. The door shuts. Action MUSIC fades down and elevator smooth jazz MUSIC fades up as COLBY enters.)

COLBY. How we doin? Good? Alright. So, Grandma Mimi and Coralee couldn't ask Randy to help find Bobbi…

(As COLBY speaks, he puts on a clerk's apron and plain men's glasses. COLBY is becoming the grocery store MANAGER.)

COLBY. That might lead back to Jim. So, they went to the local grocery to charm the manager into letting them watch his security recording. Boy, did that guy have an interesting morning.

MANAGER. Attention, shoppers. Welcome to Marvin Mart. Don't forget to check out our pulled pork in the deli and visit our bakery for a complimentary broken cookie. Our clerk Clara has been clumsy for half a century. Thank you and have a WTF day!

(MANAGER turns and "prices" a can or two on an imaginary shelf as MIMI and CORALEE walk in cautiously. MIMI takes off her sunglasses. CORALEE hangs back and spies on them while MIMI approaches the MANAGER.)

MIMI. Hello, there. Are you the manager?

MANAGER. I am. May I help you?

MIMI. Tell me, is it true you have security cameras on the parking lot and in the store?

MANAGER. It is.

MIMI. Well, my friend is missing and her car's out there. And I have reason to suspect foul play, so may I look at your recording from last night?

MANAGER. What? No! No. If you suspect foul play, I suggest you go to the police. Or, you know what? Maybe your friend's fine. And she just, you know, spent the night with another friend.

MIMI. Are you talking down to me? How dare you! I've forgotten more than you'll ever know! I need to see that recording. My friend is in danger!

MANAGER. I don't have to do anything. You need to back up! Before I call the police, OK?

(The MANAGER leaves for his office in a huff. CORALEE takes off her glasses and runs up to MIMI.)

CORALEE. Well, what now?

MIMI. Give me some time! I'm thinking. I'm thinking.

CORALEE. I don't mean to be critical, but you can catch a lot more flies with flypaper.

MIMI. You got something in mind?

CORALEE. Uh huh. Help me down and get ready to run to that office when it's empty.

(MIMI helps CORALEE lie down flat on the floor. CORALEE begins to holler before she's even on the floor.)

CORALEE. Oh, Lord! Lordy! Help! Help me! I've fallen and I can't get up!

(The MANAGER rushes out.)

MANAGER. What the? Is the floor wet? Are you OK? Please don't sue! I'll help you. I've got you. Can you get up?

(THE MANAGER tries to lift Coralee up by her shoulders as CORALEE continues to groan and holler. MANAGER can only get CORALEE to sit up. HE keeps one hand on CORALEE's back supporting her. Meanwhile, MIMI hurries behind them into his office.)

MANAGER. *(To CORALEE*) Wait a minute, weren't you with that other lady? Where is she anyway?

(MANAGER looks around as CORALEE acts confused and trembles. CORALEE stares at something invisible, stretching her arms towards the audience as the MANAGER bends down and looks where CORALEE's looking.)

CORALEE. Patrick Lee! Is that you? Back from the war? Come to Mama, baby!

(CORALEE turns, grabs and kisses the MANAGER who recoils and hollers. CORALEE stretches out her arms again as MIMI eases out of the office and stands beside CORALEE.)

CORALEE. Is that you, Dan Lee? Back from the dead?

MIMI. Sorry. Happens all the time. She forgot her medication.

MANAGER. *(Jumps up.)* You!

MIMI. What? We're just shopping.

CORALEE. I'm OK now.

MIMI. You sure? Let me help you up. We'll get you home.

MANAGER. That's a good idea. Go! And thank you for shopping at Marvin Mart.

(MANAGER exits and preps to return as COLBY.)

CORALEE. You got it?

(MIMI pulls a flash drive from her pocket and holds it up for CORALEE to see.)

MIMI. If you mean this thingamajig, yep.

CORALEE. Put that back, Mimi. Shhhh...

(MIMI pockets the drive. BOTH put on their sunglasses and look around for danger as they exit while action MUSIC plays. MIMI and CORALEE re-enter the kitchen and open up a laptop they've put on the table. MIMI's got a cell phone and thumb drive in her hand. COLBY enters with a cell phone and gets a ball cap from the prop area or brings one with

him when he enters. ACTION music fades down.)

COLBY. Grandma Mimi had a sense that things were starting to connect like a spider web. But even a spider needs help sometimes. She and Coralee borrowed a laptop from the senior center and were ready to find clues that might lead to Bobbi.

(COLBY puts the cap on backwards as he speaks. He becomes the geeky adolescent Neighbor BOY.)

MIMI. *(To Coralee)* I've got the neighbor boy on the phone to help get this do-hickey working.

BOY. *(To phone)* It's called a thumb drive, Miss Mimi. Look on the side of the keyboard. See where you plug it in?

MIMI. Got it...Done it. Now, how do I see what's on this darn fart whistle?

BOY. Press the little pad at the bottom of the keyboard in the right corner, twice.

MIMI. I think I got it.

BOY. Do you see a box with different names?

MIMI. Uh-huh. And with different dates.

BOY. Use your finger in the middle to move the little arrow to the date you want then press that pad twice and it'll play.

MIMI. Thanks for your help.

BOY. Maybe I should come over and watch to make sure there's no problems.

(CORALEE leans over and talks into MIMI's phone.)

CORALEE. You can't see this.

BOY. Why?

CORALEE. Ah, Mimi bought some porn.

BOY. Then I <u>definitely</u> wanna watch.

CORALEE. Okay, but I got to warn you. This porn's special. It's for the elderly, made by the elderly *(trying to disgust the BOY)* with old, old, ooollldd actors.

BOY. Ewwww *(Gags)* 'Scuse me. I think I got something else I need to do.

MIMI. Good call. I'll have you roll more medication tomorrow. Same deal. You get two. Bye.

(The BOY hangs up and exits. MIMI and CORALEE get ready to watch the video together.)

MIMI. OK, here goes...Yep, the video's from yesterday.

CORALEE. There's a time stamp.

MIMI. I'll nudge it up around 5. There's Bobbi going in. Looks fine, except for her hair...There she is coming out...Ok, Ok. Oh, no! Look, there's a man coming up behind her!!

CORALEE. Watch out, Bobbi!

MIMI. He's got a gun!

CORALEE. He's got Bobbi!

MIMI. He's making her get in a black Camaro. And took her, and her groceries! You suppose he's hungry?

CORALEE. I don't think so...I recognize him! That's the man who fixed my car after I got T bagged at the roundabout.

MIMI. T boned, Coralee! T boned. Come on. You know the way to his place, right? Let's go before it gets dark. He better not hurt Bobbi!

CORALEE. I'll drive.

MIMI. Good idea. I'll be right there

(CORALEE exits.)

I got to find my medicine...Oh, shoot...Where is it?

(While MIMI looks for a joint, CORALEE comes back in the doorway half-way.)

CORALEE. Hey-ay! Guess what I found coming up the walk.

(CORALEE walks in leading RANDY by the hand.)

RANDY. Hi there, Miss Mimi. Nice to see you.

MIMI. Well...My goodness! What a surprise.

CORALEE. He wants to talk to Bobbi again.

MIMI. Ohhh...Bobbi? Huh. She's not here, but, ah, please sit down, Detective. How about some pie and sweet tea?

CORALEE I'll get it. Sit down, Randy. Cool off a bit.

RANDY. OK, thanks, but I can't stay long. I'm on official business.

CORALEE. I like a man who's official.

RANDY. Well, ah, thank you, Miss Coralee. Officially, I'm looking for Bobbi. Do either of you know where she is?

MIMI. She's supposed to be making chili for the church cook-off tomorrow.

RANDY. I checked her house but she's not there.

MIMI. Maybe she's, I don't know, shopping?

RANDY. Funny you should say that. I was by Marvin Mart and the manager said two women, that sound a lot like you, were there looking for a "friend" and wanted to see his security recording, which is missing.

CORALEE. We were there! I fell in the store—

RANDY. --Are you OK?

CORALEE. Aww, that is so sweet. Did you hear that, Mimi?

MIMI. Yep. I heard.

CORALEE. Well, I'm fine but I was looking for Mimi, who is my friend, to help me up because she was there with me. That mean man said he was going to check the recording to make sure the floor wasn't wet in case I sued, which I won't. He might have done something with that video. It's evidence!

RANDY. He did say somebody fell, but—

(RANDY sniffs the air.)

MIMI. Soon as we see Bobbi or can talk to her, we'll tell her to call you. You know, she likes to be alone sometimes. She's still sad about her daughter.

RANDY. Sure, but if you see her, let her know I want to show her a picture. Here, you might as well take a look, too. You know this guy?

(RANDY pulls a photo out of his pocket and offers it to MIMI. RANDY sniffs the air in different directions--something's rotten--then RANDY takes a bite of pie while MIMI looks at the photo.)

RANDY. This pie is, mmm. It's fantastic!

CORALEE. Mine again! Sweet Potato.

RANDY. Sweet Potato? Aww, Sweet Potato. That's what my late wife used to call me. I haven't heard that in...Ah, excuse me.

(RANDY looks away, dabs his eyes and gathers himself while MIMI whispers to CORALEE.)

MIMI. It's the man in the video! Your auto shop guy.

RANDY. Sorry, what did you say?

MIMI. Sorry for your loss. And nope, can't place him.

CORALEE. This man? Is he dangerous?

RANDY. Well, I'm not sure. His name's Harry Blevins and he used to be a loan shark. He did some time at the Pensacola Prison. Harry's fixing cars now and Bobbi's son-in-law threw business his way. I'm not sure how, but I think they're mixed up together, somehow.

CORALEE. I like a man who thinks.

MIMI. Do you think Jim owes Harry money? Maybe Harry did something to Jim!

RANDY. I doubt it. Loan sharks peck at their pigeons until there's nothing to peck at. Even if Jim could only pay interest, Harry would want him around a long time.

CORALEE. So, what are you thinking?

RANDY. Now, don't get upset with me or anything, but suppose, just suppose, Jim borrowed money from the business, or maybe Harry, to help Bobbi. I heard she gambles.

MIMI. That's nuttier than a fruitcake.

RANDY. Maybe not. Everybody's got a secret side. She might have thought, "If Jim's gone, then, tah-dah! I don't have to pay him back."

CORALEE. No!

RANDY. But you heard her, Coralee. Bobbi didn't tell me about being at Jim's office. And she told you that Jim gave her pictures of Amy, but she couldn't find 'em. And somebody cleaned up Jim's office. Who had the last appointment with Jim? Bobbi!

MIMI. So you're thinking Bobbi, our Bobbi, did something bad to Jim?

RANDY. Can't rule it out. The thing is, I can't see how she could do anything like that without *(Sniffs)* help. (S*niffs again)*. Damn. Does anybody else smell something? Something foul!

(RANDY gets up and starts sniffing around the kitchen. His nose leads him towards the freezer. MIMI suddenly realizes what she did.)

MIMI. Oh, no!!

(MIMI jumps up, scrambles, and gets between RANDY and the freezer. MIMI faces RANDY, leaning back with her hands behind her on the freezer lid.)

Oh! My goodness! Bless my heart. I just remembered I did the dumbest thing. I, ah, unplugged the freezer to run the vacuum and I didn't plug it back in. I am so forgetful these days.

(CORALEE sneaks a frying pan off the wall, gets behind RANDY and holds the skillet behind her back in case she needs to keep Randy from opening the freezer.)

RANDY. *(Sniffing)* Smells like spoiled meat. Now that's a shame. I'm going right past the dump on the way home. I'd be glad to cart it off. No trouble at all.

MIMI. No. Nope. Terrible idea. The smell in the house will be worse if it's stirred up. And think what it'll do to your car. Coralee, can you plug this back in? My back's acting up.

CORALEE. Sure.

MIMI. This mess won't smell so bad when it's froze up again. We'll put it out trash day.

(CORALEE puts the skillet in front of her and bends over for Randy's benefit as she plugs in the freezer. He tries to be a gentleman and not look but doesn't succeed. When CORALEE gets up, RANDY spots the pan.)

RANDY. Why do you have a frying pan?

CORALEE. Aww, Sweet Potato. That is so cute!

(CORALEE looks deep in his eyes with an angelic smile. RANDY is transfixed until MIMI speaks and breaks the spell.)

MIMI. Is there anything else, Detective? Except Christmas cookies? Only 7 more months!

RANDY. No, but if you hear from Bobbi, or Jim or--

MIMI. --Is that your car radio? Roger. Out. Ten-Four. Yep. Sorry you got to go, but duty calls.

RANDY. If you hear anything, you've got my--

MIMI and CORALEE. Card. Yes, we'll call. Bye!

MIMI. Y'all come back now, hear?

(MIMI almost pushes RANDY out and locks the door. CORALEE puts the skillet back on the wall.)

MIMI. Coralee, we've got to get rid of Jim! The clock's ticking, maybe on Bobbi's life, and Randy's getting too many ideas. Your cowboy thinks Bobbi killed Jim and we helped her get away with it.

CORALEE. Well? That is kind of what happened.

MIMI. Don't remind me. It's too late to go by Harry's now. Since George Clooney *(or latest older heart throb)* stood me up again, go grab your things. We'll have a pajama party pow-wow. I've got an idea.

CORALEE. Oh, Mimi. I wish we could tell Randy everything so he could help find Bobbi. He's smart, and sweet and I like him. This may be my last chance to be with somebody who's a good person, and thinks I'm nice, and likes me just like I am.

MIMI. I know. And you deserve all the happiness in the world. But right now, we got to find Harry Blevins so we can find Bobbi and get her back. What do you say?

CORALEE. I say watch out Harry Blevins. Witchee Twitchee women are on the way!

(MIMI and CORALEE high five or fist bump and exit.)

COLBY. So, Harry was finding out women like Bobbi can be a handful. And Randy knew Coralee liked him, but he suspected she and Mimi were pulling a 10-gallon hat over his eyes. Our detective hoped he was wrong, but he had to find out.

(COLBY exits as RANDY sneaks in on the opposite side. NIGHT SOUNDS fade up. RANDY stops in front of MIMI's kitchen with a flashlight that he shines through a real or imaginary window towards the freezer. SOUNDS fade down.)

RANDY. I could have sworn I saw blood specks on that wall.

(CORALEE enters, sees Randy and creeps up behind him while he's still looking.)

CORALEE. Back so soon?

(RANDY,startled, turns and points his flashlight in CORALEE's eyes.)

CORALEE. Whoa there.

RANDY. Sorry about that. What are you doing out here?

CORALEE. Mimi's worried about Bobbi being missing and what you said about her. She didn't want to be alone, so I'm staying over. I heard something outside and here you are, so I should ask you the same question. What are <u>you</u> doing sneaking around outside, looking in the house?

RANDY. Well, that smell was so strong today I was concerned, for you. I mean Mimi, and you.

CORALEE. That is so nice but there's nothing to worry about. Mimi told me what the smell was.

(CORALEE circles RANDY trailing a finger over his back and around to his chest.)

RANDY. Now, don't leave me in suspense.

CORALEE. I shouldn't tell, but, since you are the law...it's my obligation to be straight-up honest with you...Mimi...killed.

RANDY. Killed? What? Who? Go ahead. Say it.

CORALEE. Mimi killed…Mimi killed a deer. She hit it with her car.

(RANDY is disappointed but relaxes.)

RANDY. Now why wouldn't she just come out and say that?

CORALEE. She was afraid. Mimi thinks it was illegal to keep the meat. Is that true?

(CORALEE gets closer and looks directly in RANDY'S eyes.)

RANDY. Out of season and not reporting it, yeah.

CORALEE. You going to arrest her?

(RANDY and CORALEE are almost chest to chest.)

RANDY. No. I like deer meat. It can be eaten in many forms. But it's very lean. I prefer something more flavorful ...juicy...full bodied.

CORALEE. My favorite is thick...sausage.

(CORALEE and RANDY are fixed on each other for a half a beat. BOTH get self-conscious and pull away.)

RANDY. Well, everything seems OK here. I should be going.

CORALEE. See you soon, Sweet Potato.

RANDY. Say, let me know if you'd like a tour of the station, maybe see where I work. There's nobody in jail right now.

CORALEE. But you may run into a very, bad, girl.

(RANDY smiles and leaves slowly. RANDY and CORALEE wiggle their fingers"bye" at each other. CORALEE sighs like a lovesick school girl when he's gone. Owl and cricket nature SOUNDS fade up.)

TO BLACK

END OF ACT II, SCENE 1

ACT II

Scene 2

Setting: Mimi's Kitchen and the Auto Body Shop later that evening.

At Rise: Nature SOUNDS stop. CORALEE is sitting at the kitchen table beside Jim's cell phone, flipping through it. MIMI is standing watching her. In the auto shop, HARRY's sitting on a chair and BOBBI's beside him, tied to the chair. The bandanna is below her chin and BOBBI's head is back with her mouth slightly open. She's sleeping and snoring softly. HARRY is flipping through his phone and drinking a beer.

(STAN enters to talk to HARRY.)

STAN. I'm going next door for a burger. Want one?

HARRY. Sure. No mustard. No onion. And bring an extra for granny.

(STAN exits. CORALEE hands MIMI Jim's phone.)

MIMI. Thank heavens Randy's sweet on you or he might have come with a search warrant.

CORALEE. And you were right. Jim's phone shows he and Harry talked almost every day.

MIMI. So, now, it's time to do this!

(MIMI dials and CORALEE stands to listen to the call. HARRY's phone RINGS. HARRY stands up, excited, looks at the screen, then answers the phone.)

HARRY. I'll be, it's Jim! Guess he's not dead after all. Hey, Jimmy Boy, where the hell you been?

MIMI. This ain't Jim, Mister..Mister Harry Blevins!

HARRY. Who's this?!

MIMI. Never you mind who I am, you warty toad frog! What's important is you are holding a friend of mine.

HARRY. I don't know what you're talking about.

MIMI. I got video from a grocery store parking lot camera that says different. You do what I say and we can both get what we want.

HARRY. Alright. Alright. I'll play along. What's your friend's name?

MIMI. You tell me who you got.

HARRY. Fair enough. Bobbi.

MIMI. That's her.

HARRY. And what do you think I want?

MIMI. I'm not playing 20 questions all night with you!

HARRY. OK. Here's the deal. I want two hundred thousand dollars, or your friend's house. Either one sets her loose. That's what her son-in-law owes.

MIMI. Jim owed you money?

HARRY. Yeah. I'm a regular guardian angel covering insurance payments he stole. He screwed up big time betting on the Dolphins.

MIMI. That was stupid! So, ah, why not go after the idiot for your money?

HARRY. Can't find him, but I found your friend and I think she got rid of her dear, sweet son-in-law.

MIMI. Listen, I don't know anything about that, but we get Bobbi back...you can have the house.

HARRY. How do you know I haven't already killed the old witch?

MIMI. You watch your potty mouth! If you did, then, we got no fish to fry. And I have the video to deliver to the police.

HARRY. Now, hold on a minute. You got no call to do that. Your friend's alive.

MIMI. Put her on.

HARRY. She's asleep.

MIMI. She snoring?

HARRY. Yeah.

MIMI. Let me hear it.

(HARRY holds the phone up to BOBBI'S face as she SNORES.)

MIMI. Yep, that's her. You bring Bobbi to me and I'll have her sign paperwork for the house.

HARRY. OK. Sure. What's the address?...Got it.

(HARRY hangs up as STAN walks in with a sack of sandwiches and a couple soft drinks. BOBBI stops SNORING, opens her eyes a bit and listens in. CORALEE and MIMI are quiet in the kitchen.)

STAN. What's up?

HARRY. I'm telling you Stan, the older women get, the stupider they are. Here. Go to this place and take whatever paperwork they've got on this 'un's house. And, before you leave, everybody there? Kill 'em.

STAN. OK, boss. *(STAN starts to leave then turns around.)* But what if they got guns?

HARRY. Yeah, it's Florida. Everybody's got guns! Well, pull yours first.

STAN. What if they don't give me the papers?

(BOBBI shuts her eyes fast and starts softly snoring again.)

HARRY. Tell them you're me, OK? That'll scare 'em into doing what you say. Harry put fear in that biddy on the phone.

STAN. Maybe because she hasn't met you in person yet. Granny here don't seem too terrified of the real deal. And what about her, once we get the goods?

HARRY. When you get back, we'll have her sign the papers, then dump her in the swamp.

STAN. You do that. I'll kill the others, but her?...OK, I'll kill her, too.

HARRY. You're gonna have some fun tonight, huh?

(HARRY starts to high five STAN and when STAN reciprocates, deliberately misses, leaves STAN hanging and laughs at him. STAN exits. BOBBI is still and HARRY sits quietly drinking his beer and looking at his phone.)

CORALEE. Why are you helping Harry get Bobbi's house? And telling him to come here?

MIMI. I had to say something.

CORALEE. Oh, Lord, a Land Shark's coming.

MIMI. Loan Shark, Coralee, Loan Shark.

CORALEE. Loan Shark, Land Shark, Shark Week. They're all bad!

MIMI. Coralee? I don't want you here when Harry comes to the house.

CORALEE. What?!

MIMI. You heard me. Bobbi's in danger and a money hungry criminal is on the way. I've put us in mortal jeopardy.

CORALEE. We are in this together, Mimi!

MIMI. But Harry may not say, "Thank you, have a nice day" if he knows the deed made out to Amy won't do him a bit of good. And he may figure out he doesn't need us to type a new one or get it signed. I'm hoping spray paint at the auto shop has fried his brain.

CORALEE. He's messed up no matter what and I cannot leave you here by yourself.

MIMI. Yes, you can, and you will. Listen, if Harry does something to both of us, you won't be around to save Bobbi, or see your own grand kids one day. And I have a feeling Randy will be heartbroken if you disappear. So please, leave. I mean it. Please.

CORALEE. I don't know.

MIMI. I'll be all right. I got this.

CORALEE. You sure?

MIMI. Sure as sugar.

CORALEE. OK, but I'm not happy about it. Oh, shoot, it's too dark to drive. I'll call a Goober.

MIMI. Uber, Coralee, Uber. And call me in an hour.

CORALEE. Bye, Mimi. Be careful. Love you.

(CORALEE blows Mimi a kiss. MIMI sends one back. When CORALEE exits, MIMI locks the door, then sits nervously at the table. Soon, there's a KNOCK at the door. MIMI opens it far enough for STAN to poke his face through the opening.)

MIMI. Are you Harry?

STAN. Does a fish swim?

MIMI. What?

STAN. *(Shouts slowly)* DOES A FI-ISH SWI-IM??

MIMI. Huh??

STAN. Jeez, stupid, old, yeah, I'm Harry!! Are you gonna let me in so we can get this done?

MIMI. You don't sound like Harry.

STAN. I sure am.

(MIMI opens the door enough that STAN can poke his upper body through the doorway.)

MIMI. Where's my friend?

STAN. In the car.

MIMI. I want to see her.

STAN. I get to see the paperwork first.

(STAN pushes the door open and MIMI back, striding in with a revolver in his hand. MIMI holds up her hands and walks backwards facing STAN, then stops.)

MIMI. Good grief. Not again!

STAN. Give me the paperwork! Now!

(STAN cocks the gun and his phone RINGS. HARRY is in the shop with his back to the audience silently on the phone with STAN. STAN keeps the gun on MIMI while he reaches for the phone with his other hand and answers it.)

STAN. Who the?...Hey...I'm getting it right now. Yeah, everything's fine. I'm not an idiot and this is not a good time to talk. Hold your horses, dude...Yeah, I'll see you soon. Bye.

(STAN pockets his phone and "Ride of the Valkyries" plays as CORALEE opens the

kitchen door and fills the door frame with her hands on her hips. The MUSIC stops as STAN turns and drops to one knee to aim at her. CORALEE grabs the frying pan from the wall by the door and STAN shoots 6 times. CORALEE whips the skillet in front of her and deflects the bullets like a Ninja. We hear RICOCHET NOISES as the bullets bounce off. STAN is out of bullets, gets up and turns to run in slow motion. CORALEE marches forward in slow motion.)

CORALEE. Bye, boy!

(CORALEE takes a batter's stance and swings at the side of Stan's head like it's a baseball. STAN sees it and says low and slow...)

STAN. OOOOOHHHH NOOOOOO!

(We hear a metal BONK when the pan connects with the side of STAN's head. STAN wilts in SLO MO, going on his knees, then wilting flat on the floor. MIMI runs up to give CORALEE a big hug.)

MIMI. Coralee, thank you for not listening to me!

CORALEE. Any time. Help me get down.

(MIMI holds an arm out for CORALEE to get on a knee and check on Stan. CORALEE looks up at MIMI.)

CORALEE. Uh, oh...I didn't mean to hit him so hard.

MIMI. I know, but you saved my life. And what's done is done.

(CORALEE gets Stan's wallet and phone.)

CORALEE. Help me up. Let's hope this one stays dead. Oh, Lord.

(CORALEE rises with MIMI's help.)

CORALEE. I haven't been this active in years. I'm gonna need a massage!

(CORALEE hands MIMI the wallet.)

And this isn't the guy who fixed my car. He's not Harry, that's for sure.

(MIMI takes money out of the wallet and looks at the ID)

MIMI. He sure isn't. He lied! His name's Stan. What is wrong with these people? Have they no respect for the 10 commandments? At least he's got money for that massage.

(MIMI gives CORALEE the money, gives STAN a little kick, and throws the wallet on his stomach.)

MIMI. I'm calling that yellow chicken Harry-coward right now.

(CORALEE gives STAN's foot a nudge, too.)

CORALEE. OK. Don't wait on me. I'll be right back.

(CORALEE exits. MIMI sits at the Kitchen Table with Stan's phone. She is still. Before MIMI makes her call, we're back in the Auto Shop. BOBBI watches HARRY rummage through his fast-food sack. HARRY pulls out a couple of burger containers, sets them down and jerks the bandanna below BOBBI'S mouth.)

BOBBI. What now?

HARRY. You hungry? Got you a burger.

BOBBI. Please, no more fast food! That stuff 'll kill ya'. Besides, I've got diverticulitis.

HARRY. Diver tickles your what?

BOBBI. Never mind. Why are you being nice getting me something to eat?

HARRY. *(Mouth full)* MMND NNNNM a nnnn bbbhhh

BOBBI. What?

HARRY. phhhmm maah mull hhhn.

BOBBI. What?

HARRY. *(Swallows)* I said, consider it your last meal.

BOBBI. Why? You letting me go?

HARRY. My boy Stan went to your friend's house to get the deed to your house. When he gets back, you're gonna sign it. Only way you're gonna keep breathing.

BOBBI. I don't believe you. I think you're going to kill me.

HARRY. It makes no difference to me what you think.

(MIMI uses Stan's phone to call HARRY, who is enjoying his sandwich. His phone RINGS.)

HARRY. Well, well, well. Here's Stan a callin' now. How about I put him on speaker so you can hear what happened to your friends in all its glory. Talk to me, Stan!

MIMI. Your asshole friend is dead.

(HARRY's in shock. BOBBI's ecstatic as she shouts to the phone.)

BOBBI. Mimi! Come get me! This jerk's trying to kill me with fast food.

(CORALEE bursts in through the Kitchen door, not bothering to close it. She is holding a chain saw she revs from IDLE to CUT speed then back to IDLE as she moves towards MIMI's phone. HARRY looks at his phone like it's poison. The women play it up and shout into MIMI's phone for HARRY'S benefit.)

MIMI. Turn off that thing. I'm trying to have a conversation.

CORALEE. Bad timing, I'm trying to chop this guy up.

(Chain saw NOISE stops and CORALEE puts the saw down.)

BOBBI. My friends! Ain't they grand?

HARRY. What did you do to Stan?

MIMI. Same thing he was going to do to us!

HARRY. Listen, lady--

MIMI. --No, you listen. We want our friend back. You better not hurt a hair on her head or the police see the video.

HARRY. OK, you wanna play hardball? Well, let's play. Forget about the video and the house. It's off the table. You give me 200 grand. No, now it's three hundred thousand *(Raise whatever price you've used for the house.)* if you want your friend back alive. You've got 24 hours or else. *(HARRY, then MIMI, hangs up).*

CORALEE. Oh. Lord. Here we go again. All I've got is the massage money and maybe $600 until I get my Social Security check.

MIMI. We'll think of something. We have to. First, we gotta get rid of Jim and Stan. My freezer's full. And our favorite detective is playing connect-the-dots.

CORALEE. What'll we do?

MIMI. *(Thinks, then after a beat or two...)* I've got it. Tomorrow morning, I'm taking a ride. And after I leave, you're getting Randy over here. Give him something to do. Then you take off and let's meet up behind Harry's shop, say about 10. We don't want Randy showing up there until we want him to. Let's see, I need Jim and Stan's phones and I'll write a note for Bobbi.

CORALEE. You've lost me.

MIMI. I'll explain I all over a glass of pinot nor-ee, while we make some mon-ey.

(Mimi looks down at Stan and gives him another little kick.)

That OK with you Stan? *(In low voice)* "S'alright."

(Action MUSIC fades up)

TO BLACK

END OF ACT II, SCENE 2

ACT II

Scene 3

Setting: The next morning in Mimi's Kitchen and the Auto Shop.

At Rise: BOBBI is tied in her chair with the bandanna below her mouth, sleeping in the Auto Shop. We see RANDY--wearing a frilly apron over his jeans--working beside CORALEE at Mimi's kitchen table. They are chopping vegetables. The MUSIC fades as COLBY enters and continues his story.

COLBY. I was getting in town that night to spend a week with Grandma. Her life had turned into a three-ring circus but Grandma was determined to have a special meal for me. No Jim, Stan, Harry or Randy was getting between her and her grandson. But Mimi's optimism everything would go fine was kind of cross-eyed.

RANDY. *(Singing slowly, chopping vegetables)*. One way, or another I'm gonna find y'a, I'm gonna get ya, gonna get ya, get ya, get ya, get ya...

CORALEE. Sure is nice on your day off to help us get ready for dinner tonight.

RANDY. Glad to...Say, I read in Cosmopolitan--

CORALEE. You read Cosmo?

RANDY. It was the only magazine at the laundromat. Anyway, it said women are, you know, attracted, to men who cook.

CORALEE. Works for me.

RANDY. Wait 'til you see me scrub a tub!

CORALEE. Ooooh, you know the way to a woman's heart. And I bet you're good at any *(looks him up and down)* thing you put your mind to. You know they say when you do something new for the first time, it's best to go…slow…

(RANDY'S leg visible to the audience starts to shake. He pushes down on it as a brake while looking at CORALEE sweetly, hoping she doesn't notice.)

CORALEE: Hey, Colby's going to think you're the berries. And all this special food! Not every day a good-looking lawman helps make a meal.

RANDY. I used to help my wife cook. This brings back happy times, and good memories.

CORALEE. I'm glad. Truly.

RANDY. Me too...Say, where's Mimi?

CORALEE. Oh, she had errands to run. In fact, I got to meet her right now and help out. Now chop those onions fine and when you're through dicing and slicing, let yourself out. I'll finish up when I get back.

(CORALEE pulls a bulky bag from under the table or out of a kitchen cabinet. RANDY stares at her.)

RANDY. What's in the bag?

CORALEE. It's full of money.

RANDY. Seriously.

CORALEE. Shoot, I don't have enough cash to start a fire. Mimi's always got some arts and crafts supplies for the senior center. I'll see you tonight...Sweet Potato.

RANDY. I'll miss you.

CORALEE. Oooh, you better watch out saying such stuff. I always get my man.

(CORALEE gives RANDY a big smile and leaves with her bag. As soon as the door closes, suspenseful MUSIC plays as RANDY takes off his apron, puts the cutting board aside, and walks slyly to the freezer. He looks around, opens the top, and sticks as much of his body as he can inside. MUSIC stops. RANDY comes back up and turns around towards the audience, astonished. A suspenseful MUSICAL phrase plays. RANDY speaks.)

RANDY. I can't believe it! Pecans? Cake? I thought....Am I disappointed, or not. Dang! I wish she'd stop calling me Sweet Potato!

(RANDY closes the freezer, grabs his hat and exits. In the Auto Shop, BOBBI's in her chair looking around. BOBBI hears HARRY enter and pretends to be asleep. HARRY pokes BOBBI on the shoulder.)

HARRY. Wake up old woman.

BOBBI. Whaa?... I gotta use the bathroom.

HARRY. Hold it. Your friends are gonna be here soon. Wish they'd hurry up.

(We hear metallic CLATTERS and a couple loud THUMPS off stage.)

HARRY. What was that noise? Sounds like something in the alley.

BOBBI. Probably all your hopes and dreams going in the dumpster.

HARRY. You just can't keep a lid on it can you?

BOBBI. Sure I can. Watch.

(BOBBI purses her lips and looks Harry up and down, studying every detail.)

HARRY. What are you doing?

BOBBI. You know, I've seen a lot of you lately and I've been thinking.

HARRY. Why would you do that for?

BOBBI. You're not that bad looking.

HARRY. Don't look at me that way. Ever.

BOBBI. I'm not. But you could really use a make-over. New hairstyle, new wardrobe, the whole bit.

HARRY. I look fine!

BOBBI. When was the last time you were with a woman?

HARRY. When was the last time you been with a man?

BOBBI. I'm old, wrinkled and been divorced many years. It happened back in the Clinton administration, *(Or any presidential term about 20 years before the present.)* when your clothes were in style.

HARRY. Shut up! When I want advice on how to dress, I'll ask Waylon Jennings.

BOBBI. Waylon Jennings reminds me of Stan. They're both dead.

(HARRY grabs the bandana and pulls it over Bobbi's mouth as BOBBI protests. Harry leans in close.)

HARRY. I am so tired of you. You know what? When your son-in-law, Jim, ran over your daughter, he should a waited 'til you were with her...and killed the both of ya.

(BOBBI is horrified.)

HARRY. So, you didn't know, did you? Huh. Well, if you did something to Jim, he had it coming but it would a been better if you'd a waited until after I got my money.

(HARRY's phone BUZZES and he looks at the message, then at BOBBI.)

HARRY. There, there, it'll all be over soon. The old coots are parking. It's show time!

(HARRY pulls a gun from the back of his pants and checks to make sure it's loaded while BOBBI glares at him. MIMI and CORALEE, carrying the money bag, enter and stand "outside" the shop.)

CORALEE. Did you send those text messages from Stan's phone before the dumpster deposit?

MIMI. Yep, and here's what <u>you</u> gotta give Bobbi so she'll understand what <u>she</u> needs to say.

(MIMI hands a piece of paper to CORALEE.)

CORALEE. I got your back, darlin'.

MIMI. And I got yours.

(MIMI and CORALEE stand outside the shop, nervously waiting. BOBBI tries to say something before HARRY goes out to meet them.)

BOBBI. mf ggh uun, mf gggh uuunnn

HARRY. What now?

BOBBI. Mf gghh, fees gt unnnn!

HARRY. I'm gonna regret this, but what the hell.

(HARRY pulls down BOBBI'S bandana.)

BOBBI. He's got a gun!! He's got a gun!!

HARRY. Can it. They can't hear you no way. Now, I got work to do.

(HARRY pulls the bandana up over BOBBI's mouth and walks cautiously out towards MIMI and CORALEE, a gun in one hand, as the WOMEN watch him. HARRY stops and invites the women with a gesture to make the next move.)

MIMI. Are you the real Mr. Harry Blevins?

HARRY. You're looking at him.

MIMI. Well, we're here. We got your money.

CORALEE. Show us Bobbi.

(HARRY walks backwards cautiously to the shop "door," watching the women. He opens the door. BOBBI sits up straight and starts mumbling excitedly. MIMI and CORALEE nod and smile at her as HARRY closes the door and walks them back "out" slowly.)

HARRY. Now, open that bag.

(CORALEE opens it and shows him the top of the bag from a distance.)

HARRY. Toss me one of those bundles.

MIMI. Go ahead. Do what he says.

(MIMI gets at least halfway behind CORALEE. CORALEE throws a bundle of bills on the ground in front of HARRY. HARRY glances at the money, then points his gun on the women.)

HARRY. Now don't run. If you do, you're leaving your friend to die. Put the bag down and shove it here.

(MIMI peeks around CORALEE who pushes or kicks the bag towards HARRY. HARRY

takes out a bundle of bills, keeping the gun on the women as he flips through it with his thumb. There's a bill on the top and the bottom with white paper in between. HARRY stands and slips off the rubber band holding the bundle together with disgust and lets white paper float down as he starts to laugh.)

HARRY. Putting bills on top of paper? Really? People only get away with that in the movies. Just how dumb do you think I am?

CORALEE. Well, from what we know about Stan and Jim, seems like you're king of the stupid club.

HARRY. That's it. I don't get my money, and you don't get to live.

(HARRY levels the gun at CORALEE and cocks the trigger. MIMI pulls a gun out of her waistband, steps to the side of CORALEE and shoots. BANG SFX! HARRY flings his gun away.)

Owww! My shootin' hand.

(HARRY lunges towards MIMI who fires at one of Harry's feet.

My kickin' foot! Owww!

HARRY starts hopping and hollering while CORALEE picks up his gun and points it at him.)

CORALEE. Stay still and put your hands up.

(RANDY rushes in. RANDY throws on the brakes and takes in the scene, gun drawn. He's not sure who's the bad guy so he alternates aiming at Mimi, Coralee, and Harry. CORALEE grins and waves at him with one

hand as MIMI carefully raises one hand and lowers her gun to the ground with the other.)

RANDY. What the? Coralee! Mimi! Harry! Coralee??

MIMI. Thank goodness. You can put that gun down, Coralee. It's our knight in denim armor.

CORALEE. Happy to!

(CORALEE puts her gun hand down.)

RANDY. Hands behind your back, Harry. Turn around and don't move.

(HARRY hops around backwards, favoring his hurt foot and holding hands behind him.)

MIMI. *(To RANDY)* Can you get Bobbi? She's inside.

RANDY. That's exactly why I came here! But I can't be in two places at once. Coralee Campbell! I hereby deputize you.

(CORALEE salutes RANDY, runs up to give him a peck on the cheek and hands RANDY her gun. HARRY turns back around.)

CORALEE. Yes, sir. I accept. You want me to sit on him?

RANDY. No! Use this.

(RANDY gives the gun back to CORALEE.)

CORALEE. With pleasure!

(CORALEE points the gun at Harry. MIMI pushes the money bag to the side so RANDY won't see it, picks up her gun and puts it back in her waistband as RANDY finds a happy BOBBI inside. RANDY unties her and helps BOBBI up.)

BOBBI. Randall McLemore, I am so happy to see you.

(BOBBI pinches RANDY's cheek then gives it a peck before they walk out.)

RANDY. Ow! You're welcome, I think. I haven't had kisses from two women in one day for a long time.

BOBBI. I am so happy to be out of that place. *(To HARRY)* You! You made me miss my hair appointment. And the chili contest! *(To RANDY)* Say, how did you know I was here?

RANDY. I got a text from Stan, that guy who works for Harry.

(CORALEE gets close to BOBBI and hands her a note. BOBBI reads it and nods that she understands as the others talk. She gets rid of the note, i.e., stuffs the note in her cleavage or pretends to wad it up and swallow it.)

HARRY. What?

MIMI. I'll be. Stan let us know where Bobbi was, too!

HARRY. Stan texted you both? Wait a minute. He's dead. So's Jim.

RANDY. Nobody said Jim or Stan is dead.

HARRY. Well, they are. And they did it. It was them! Them wicked, wicked women! They're dangerous, I'm telling ya. You better lock 'em up.

MIMI. Look, Randy.

(MIMI pulls out her cell phone to show RANDY. HARRY sidles in to look, too.)

Here's the last thing Stan sent to my phone. "Battery dying. So am I. Harry got me. Check the dumpster if you can't find me."

RANDY. *(To MIMI)* Wait a gosh darn minute. How'd Stan get your number? And mine?

BOBBI. Why from me! Stan tried to help me get away from numb nuts. He even untied me once. He was real nice. And that’s the truth.

(BOBBI gives MIMI a thumbs up as RANDY talks to CORALEE.)

RANDY. Coralee, keep this guy covered. I smell something!

(CORALEE speaks as RANDY hurries off stage.)

CORALEE. Take your time. I'm good.

HARRY. *(Turns around.)* The noise in the alley. The phones. The texts. I can't believe a gang of, of, grandmas set me up! I swear, I am going to get every one of you. And that's no threat. That's a Harry Blevins promise.

MIMI. You'll be a lot better off promising to stay far away from us. We didn't start this but we'll finish it if you don't change your ways, mister. And don't think we can't. Sending Stan to do your dirty work. Shame on you.

BOBBI. I hope you get nothing but greasy fast food in jail.

CORALEE. We're having a real nice fish fry tonight.

BOBBI. Broil mine. Please.

(RANDY enters again, gun drawn.)

RANDY. I'll take over, Coralee.

CORALEE. Yes, Sir!

(CORALEE puts the gun down.)

RANDY. Harry Blevins, you're under arrest for double murder. Miss Bobbi. I'm so sorry but I'm pretty sure your son-in-law, Jim, or most of him, is in the dumpster, with Stan, their wallets and phones.

BOBBI. My son-in-law. A heap of garbage! What a shame.

(RANDY grabs HARRY by a shoulder and turns to lead him away at gunpoint. RANDY stops as MIMI speaks.)

MIMI. You are still joining us for dinner tonight, Detective, aren't you? I already told my grandson you were coming and now, we sure do have reason to celebrate. You saved us, rescued our friend and caught a heinous criminal. The least we can do is feed you. And Coralee will be so disappointed if you don't come. I've never seen her happier than when you're around.

CORALEE. Mimi! I was playing hard to get!

RANDY. You are not good at fooling anybody about anything, Coralee. See you later, Ladies.

(RANDY exits, pushing a limping HARRY in front of him.)

CORALEE. *(To Bobbi)* Let's get you home so you can get cleaned up and ready for tonight.

MIMI. You feeling up to it?

BOBBI. Does a fish swim?

MIMI. If its name ain't Stan. I'm running to the airport to get Colby. See you tonight.

(Cheerful MUSIC plays.)

TO BLACK

END OF ACT II, SCENE 3

ACT II

Scene 4

Setting: That evening in Mimi's kitchen.

At Rise: CORALEE, RANDY, and BOBBI are at the kitchen table. They're sipping on margaritas. MIMI is standing nearby. COLBY is on stage. JIM's desk and the auto shop chairs have been pushed against a wall, if the stage is small, to create more space.

COLBY. When I got to Grandma's, I was looking forward to freedom and fun for three sweet summer weeks. It started with a great celebration that night. I had a fine time. Randy let me mess with the siren in his patrol car and Bobbi showed me how to use something called "product" on my hair. For dinner, there was fried catfish, cornbread, coleslaw, Bobbi's green bean casserole, sweet tea and dessert. Coralee slipped me an extra piece of sweet potato pie. I ate it on the porch swing and caught tree frogs on the window screen. In front of that open window, I listened the very first time while the grownups talked.

RANDY. I cannot you are all so calm and relaxed after everything that happened today. You don't seem upset, or worried or nothin'.

MIMI. Why should we be? We've got you right here.

RANDY. Harry cursed you in my patrol car all the way to the station. I don't know if he's got anybody else working for him so I'll have officers drive by for a couple weeks to check on you. If you hear anything--

MIMI, BOBBI & CORALEE. We've got your card. We'll call!

RANDY. You were so lucky. If there is a next time, which I hope there ain't ever, promise you'll let me handle any low life botherin' you.

(MIMI, BOBBI, & CORALEE cross their hearts and raise their glasses to RANDY.)

MIMI. You bet.

BOBBI. I'll say.

CORALEE. You saved us!

RANDY. Well, no thanks necessary. Just doing my job. And you know what? I suspect Harry lent Jim money.

BOBBI. I'll be. You're absolutely right. Harry told me Jim stole insurance payments. To bet on the Dolphins!

RANDY. The Dolphins? That was stupid! So, maybe Jim was gonna get rid of Harry. That way Jim didn't have to pay Harry back. If Harry suspected that, well, Harry had to protect himself and take Jim out. And Stan, he was a witness to everything. Guess he had to go, too. Harry's a mean man. Worse, and I hate to bring this up, Bobbi, but I suspect Jim had something to do with your darlin' daughter's death.

BOBBI. If he did, his maker knows and Jim's facing him now. What goes around, comes around.

CORALEE. That's caramel.

MIMI. That's karma, Coralee...Oh, don't pay any attention. You're absolutely right.

BOBBI. Randy, how'd you like dinner?

RANDY. It was wonderful. Everything's wonderful. In fact, I'd like to make a toast....I'm grateful and glad I met a such wonderful gal with such fine upstanding friends.

CORALEE Awww. You are so sweet. And, who wants another margarita? Me! Mimi, where's the ice?

MIMI. I'll get it.

(MIMI goes to the freezer, opens the lid, pulls out an ice tray and closes the lid. Then, with a sly grin, she turns back, lifts the lid and speaks to the inside of the freezer.)

MIMI. You OK in there?

CORALEE and BOBBI. Mimi!!

MIMI. What??

(From the freezer interior, we hear a deep VOICE. "S'alright." Everyone smiles, and then is quiet. MIMI walks to Center Stage as COLBY speaks.)

COLBY. Later that year, Grandma and Coralee planted gardenias in Bobbi's backyard in Amy's memory.

(BOBBI and CORALEE walk forward and join hands with MIMI.)

COLBY. Next year, when those gardenias bloomed, Coralee and Randy exchanged their vows.

(RANDY walks up and takes CORALEE's other hand. She disengages to swat a "bug" away from his face as RANDY ducks.)

COLBY. Bobbi got a minister's license on cheap clergy certificate dot com and did the honors. Coralee's daughter and my mom were bridesmaids. When me and her were leaving, mom begged Grandma to move in with us. Just like every year, Grandma said, "not yet." Harry? He got life in prison. One day, he escaped, made it to the nearest gas station and asked how to get to Witchee Twitchee. He was last seen hitchhiking in the exact opposite direction! They say, though, when the moon is full, you can see a man on the other side of the tracks dancing with a broom.

(The "Sleeping Beauty Waltz" plays as STAN dances out with his broom and then exits dancing as the MUSIC fades. STAN preps to return quickly as JIM by taking off his ball cap, wiping off his tooth blacking and putting Jim's bloody shirt over Stan's.)

COLBY. Grandma Mimi told me he used to work for Harry. She told me a lot of other things, too...

(COLBY joins the line next to MIMI and gives her a quick shoulder hug while MIMI smiles proudly.)

COLBY. Like never bet on the Dolphins...

(JIM walks out eating from the thrown-out casserole dish, acknowledging us with a wave of his fork as JIM joins the line.)

COLBY. And always be nice to your mother-in-law! Two more things I learned from Grandma...you can use a skillet to cook a goose...and always, always, always, keep your freezer cold. Night y'all.

(Cheerful MUSIC plays.)

TO BLACK

THE END

ABOUT THE AUTHOR

Kathy McSteen began performing stand-up comedy at age 65. That adventure was sidelined by the 2020 Covid pandemic. Early into the shutdown, Kathy watched the indie film *Bad Grandmas.* She says, "I was convinced before I even finished the movie that it had the bones for an entertaining play." The film's authors and creative team were delighted to see their work evolve. With their support and workshopping," Grandma's" took flight. "If I can make people laugh and help them forget their troubles with anything I do or create, then mission accomplished." Kathy is a member of the Sarasota Area Playwright's Society and The Dramatists Guild. She continues to write while performing stand-up and producing comedy shows throughout SW Florida.

Made in the USA
Middletown, DE
21 January 2025